100 CHARACTERS FROM
CLASSICAL MYTHOLOGY

DISCOVER THE FASCINATING STORIES OF THE GREEK AND ROMAN DEITIES

MALCOLM DAY

A Quarto book

First edition for North America
published in 2007 by Barron's
Educational Series, Inc.

All inquiries should be addressed to:
Barron's Educational Series, Inc.
250 Wireless Boulevard
Hauppauge, NY 11788
www.barronseduc.com

ISBN-10: 0-7641-6006-0
ISBN-13: 978-0-7641-6006-6

Library of Congress Control Number
2006932166

QUAR.MYF

Conceived, designed, and produced by
Quarto Inc.
The Old Brewery
Blundell Street
London
N7 9BH

Project Editor **Donna Gregory**
Art Editor **Elizabeth Healey**
Assistant Art Director **Penny Cobb**
Text Editor **Diana Chambers**
Picture Researcher **Claudia Tate**
Indexer **Sue Edwards**

Art Director **Moira Clinch**
Publisher **Paul Carslake**

Manufactured by Universal Graphics
(PTE) Ltd, Singapore
Printed by Midas Printing International
Ltd, China

Printed in China
987654321

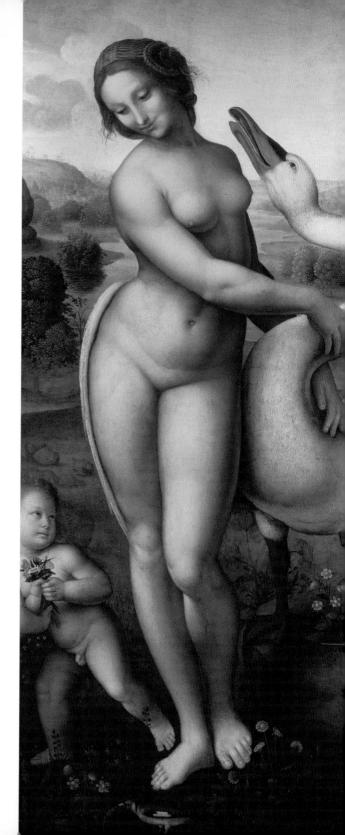

CONTENTS

INTRODUCTION

Two things above all others shaped Greek civilization and the remarkable mythology that arose from it: landscape and language. The geography of Greece forced the ancient Greeks to become seafarers; no Mediterranean country was so exposed to the sea. And since Greece's rugged interior virtually closed off its mainland from the European continent, its people were reliant on sail and oar for communication.

The mountains and broken coastline of Greece divided up the mainland into areas which became small kingdoms, each enclosed by natural barriers. This pattern was followed almost exactly by the city-states that came into being from the eighth century BCE onwards. The aristocratic families of these city-states constructed genealogies that linked them with legendary heroes associated with the cities. Landscape, then, had the effect of creating a number of separate myths linked to early settlements. Places such as Sparta, Mycenae, Tiryns, Athens, Thebes, Corinth, and Argos appear in story after story.

The second factor that shaped the mythology of the ancient Greeks was the language itself. The subtlety and range of the Greek tongue encouraged speculation about the nature of existence. Human endeavor so often depended for its success on the forces of nature, which could so easily dash the efforts of the mightiest of heroes. Poets such as Homer, in *The Iliad* and *The Odyssey*, delighted their audiences with tales of the Trojan War and other great adventures, recounting how godly intervention determined the outcome of human entanglements. The trials and tribulations of these characters explore the gamut of universal themes—love, jealousy, anger, sorrow, power, ambition, deceit, beauty, suffering, destiny, and fate—all play their part in a kind of primitive science, in which colorful legends offer an explanation of the world and all that happens in it.

The philosopher Plato (427–347 BCE) was the first Greek to use the word mythologia. By myth, he meant the telling of stories containing only invented figures. Later thinkers argued that the Greek myths and legends related to historical events, and that the gods were originally men who had distinguished themselves and who, after their death, received divine honors from a grateful people.

In the seventh century BCE, the poet Hesiod felt the need to put Greek mythology into some kind of order. His great poem *Theogony* was the first attempt at constructing genealogies tracing descent from primordial gods to heroes. Centuries later, Apollodorus drew up a comprehensive span of the entire mythical history of ancient Greece, from the origins of the universe and the gods to the Trojan War and its aftermath. The family trees presented in this book combine these sources, giving the most common renderings of the classical myths.

As for the emergence of Roman mythology, the influence of Greece was all important. The early Greek colonies in Sicily and on the Italian peninsula introduced the Romans to a more developed mythology than they themselves possessed. The Roman conquest of Greece in the second century BCE completed the process of assimilation and made the Greek and Roman gods almost indistinguishable. Jupiter came to be thought of as Zeus, just as Mars and Minerva were identified with the Greek deities, Ares and Athena, and they acquired many of their attributes and myths too. The merging of the pantheons was assisted by the fact that the Romans had never thought of their gods in human terms but saw them, rather, as personifications of natural forces. The sheer variety and human concerns of Greek myths and legends therefore entranced the Romans.

Only in one instance did Rome maintain its mythological independence. This was in the story of its founder hero Aeneas. To assert the antiquity of the Romans, and yet remain at a comfortable distance from the glories of the ancient Greeks, Aeneas was portrayed as a Trojan. His flight from the Greek sack of Troy became the starting point of Roman history.

PART I
GODS & GODDESSES

It was the poet Hesiod who first put order into Greek mythology. His epic poem Theogony, drew up the earliest account of the origins of the gods and mortals. Within this great scheme, he designed an entire genealogy that showed the linear development from the first forces of creation to the Olympian gods who were worshiped in the eighth century BCE.

To the ancient Greeks, the gods of Mount Olympus ruled the world, but they had not always done so. Oral traditions spoke of other gods and primeval forces that existed at an earlier time when the universe was in its infancy. In many cases, the myths that tell of these earlier gods fulfilled the role of explaining the existence of nature. Hesiod created a huge, intricate family tree with numerous branches to explain the interrelationship of the gods and goddesses. The idea of a family of gods was a common theme in the ancient world. Intermarriage and the production of grotesque offspring are regular features.

Three main strata of this cosmology can be discerned. The primordial gods represent the elements of the universe: day, night, earth, sea, sky, and so on. From these divinities issued the Titans, a more personified group of deities whose raison d'être was to explain the physical features of the world, such as mountains and oceans, and the beginnings of the present generation of gods.

The focus of the Titans' struggle was the rise of Zeus to the highest position in the Greek pantheon. In it he recounts the god's rebellion against his father Cronus, leader of the Titans. It is with the generation after the Titans that distinct characters of the gods began to develop.

Much of the mythology relates to Zeus and his many children with women and goddesses. Reference is frequently made to the anger of Hera, Zeus' wife, at these liaisons. But behind this conflict may have been a historical event only faintly remembered by the ancient Greeks: their original settlement of the mainland and the Aegean Islands. Some of the legends preserved indicate the existence of early deities that were subsumed into later mythology. Their uneasy marriage was the result of a sky father's cult being imposed on that of a well-established earth mother. The complexity and repetition of the theme in the legends as we have received them may partly be explained by this process of mythical accretion.

PRIMORDIAL

GODS

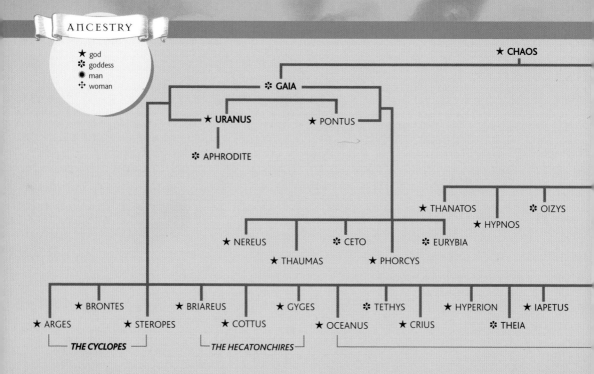

ANCESTRY

★ god
❁ goddess
✹ man
✢ woman

★ **CHAOS**

❁ **GAIA**

★ **URANUS**   ★ PONTUS

❁ APHRODITE

★ THANATOS   ❁ OIZYS

★ HYPNOS

★ NEREUS   ❁ CETO   ❁ EURYBIA

★ THAUMAS   ★ PHORCYS

★ BRONTES   ★ BRIAREUS   ★ GYGES   ❁ TETHYS   ★ HYPERION   ★ IAPETUS

★ ARGES   ★ STEROPES   ★ COTTUS   ★ OCEANUS   ★ CRIUS   ❁ THEIA

THE CYCLOPES   *THE HECATONCHIRES*

Chaos existed before all creation, at a time when the elements of the Earth were still without order. Out of Chaos were born Nyx (Night), Erebus (Underground Darkness), and Gaia (Earth). From Gaia's union with her son Uranus (Sky) came the mighty Titans and Titanesses, the earliest generation of deities. In the ensuing cosmological struggle between the Titans and their father Uranus, the Titans seized power and fathered the next generation of gods—the Olympians.

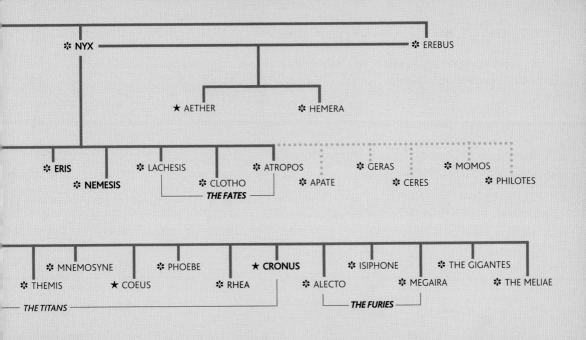

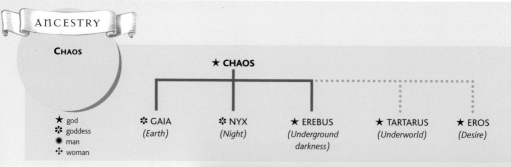

CHAOS

★ **CHAOS**

★ god
❋ goddess
✳ man
✥ woman

❋ **GAIA**
(Earth)

❋ **NYX**
(Night)

★ **EREBUS**
(Underground darkness)

★ **TARTARUS**
(Underworld)

★ **EROS**
(Desire)

C H A O S

The formless void out of which sprang Night, Day, and Earth.

In the Olympian myth of creation, Chaos produced Gaia (Earth), Nyx (Night), and Erebus (Underground Darkness). In the next phase of creation, Gaia gave birth to Uranus (Sky) and Pontus (Sea).

However, according to the system of genealogy devised in the ancient tradition of Hesiod, other offspring of Chaos included Tartarus (the Underworld), Eros (Desire), and Gaia in the first phase of the creation of the deities. Eros consorted with Chaos and caused the generative process whereby creatures, such as birds and beasts, were created.

Hesiod gave few details concerning the nature of Chaos. The Roman poet Ovid, however, described Chaos as lifeless matter, a conglomeration of all the elements with no distinguishing features, and said that Desire (or Cupid in Roman mythology) caused the first generation of identifiable creatures.

OTHER PHILOSOPHIES
Many philosophers considered primal Chaos to be the foundation of all reality. Heraclitus believed fire to be the primordial element, while the Orphic schools favored some sort of creative urge, as represented by Eros and Aphrodite, at the

FORMLESS VOID *Chaos as a churning expanse with mythological figures mingling and colliding.*

foundation of the universe. Aristotle developed his concept of *prima materia* (the formless base of all matter), a concept later adopted by alchemists.

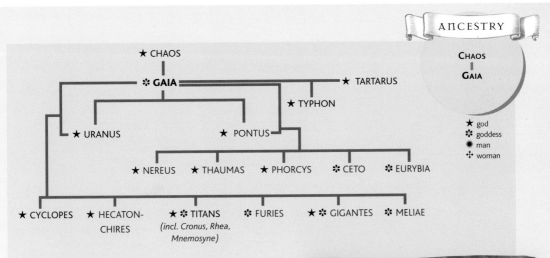

★ CHAOS

❊ GAIA ═══════════ ★ TARTARUS

★ TYPHON

★ URANUS ★ PONTUS

★ NEREUS ★ THAUMAS ★ PHORCYS ❊ CETO ❊ EURYBIA

★ CYCLOPES ★ HECATON-
CHIRES
★ ❊ TITANS
(incl. Cronus, Rhea, Mnemosyne)
❊ FURIES ★ ❊ GIGANTES ❊ MELIAE

CHAOS
|
GAIA

★ god
❊ goddess
✳ man
✢ woman

GAIA

Mother Earth, the first-born child of Chaos.

Gaia (Earth) gave birth to Uranus (Sky) and Pontus (Sea) without a father. From Uranus' fertile rain that fell lovingly on Gaia, she produced grass, flowers, trees, and the birds and beasts. She was famous for her oracles and prophecies, and was believed to have founded the oracular shrine at Delphi.

From her union with Uranus, Gaia gave birth to the monstrous Cyclopes. Then she bore the first generation of the gods, the Titans, who included Cronus and Rhea, the parents of Zeus. When Cronus proved to be tyrannical, just like his father Uranus, Gaia prophesied that one of his sons would usurp him. To prevent this happening, Cronus swallowed all his children except one—his third son, Zeus. As soon as the baby was born,

Rhea smuggled him (with Gaia's help) to Crete, where he was hidden in a cave and brought up by nymphs.

When the second generation of gods, the Olympians, ruled the world, Gaia mated with Tartarus and gave birth to the monster Typhon, a hundred-headed creature with a snake's tail who challenged Zeus. Many battles ensued but eventually Zeus was the victor.

The castration of Uranus by Cronus caused the eternal separation of the earth from the sky, and from Uranus' spilled blood and semen Gaia gave birth to the Furies, nymphs, and various giants. She also produced Mnemosyne, "Memory," through whom she passed on her

MOTHER GODDESS *Bronze portal showing Gaia suckling her children. Also shown is the sea goddess Thalassa, in some traditions the daughter of Aether and Hemera.*

knowledge to her grand-daughters, the Muses.

In Roman mythology, the equivalent Earth goddess was Tellus, who represented peace and prosperity.

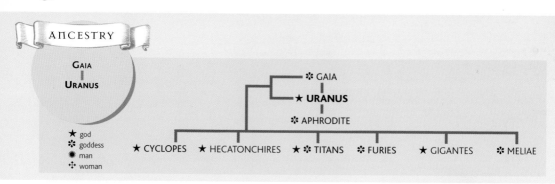

GAIA
|
URANUS

✦ god
❋ goddess
☀ man
✢ woman

❋ GAIA
|
★ URANUS
|
❋ APHRODITE

★ CYCLOPES　★ HECATONCHIRES　★ ❋ TITANS　❋ FURIES　★ GIGANTES　❋ MELIAE

URANUS

The first sky god.

In the beginning, Gaia (Earth) emerged from Chaos and in her sleep gave birth to Uranus without the aid of a man. His name is the male form of the Greek Ur-ana, meaning "queen of the mountains," and so he resided in the mountains gazing down lovingly on his mother. Uranus fed her with life-giving rain that formed the rivers and lakes, which she used to produce all the elements of nature.

Uranus and his mother mated, and from their union the race of Titans and Titanesses was born. Before their birth, however, Uranus and Gaia produced three monstrous sons, the Cyclopes, who rebelled against their father and were thrown into the abyss of Tartarus as a punishment. One tradition maintains that Gaia's maternal instinct drove her to take revenge on Uranus by persuading their other sons, the Titans, to attack him. A more orthodox version says that Uranus enveloped Gaia with his unceasing love so that her children were all imprisoned within her womb. Her youngest son Cronus decided to release his siblings by slaying his father.

CASTRATION OF URANUS
Gaia gave Cronus, her youngest son, a flint sickle so that she would be avenged. Creeping up on Uranus while he slept, Cronus grabbed his father's genitals and castrated him, then cast the bloody organs into the sea. Afterwards, the Titan brothers descended to Tartarus and rescued the Cyclopes.

One legend recounts that Aphrodite, goddess of love, emerged from among the foam gathering around the genitals that floated on the sea. Another story says that the drops of blood flowing from Uranus' wound fell on Gaia and from them were born the Furies, three female avengers of wrong who pursued those guilty of crimes commited within a family.

URANUS AS PRIMORDIAL GOD
This fresco shows Uranus as a bountiful, important deity. The stars above the heads of Uranus and his children signify their status as deities.

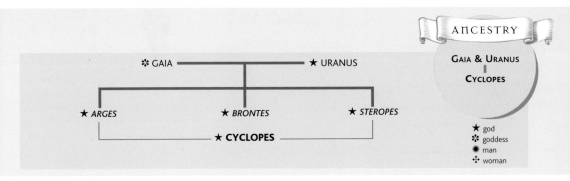

✤ GAIA ──────── ★ URANUS

★ ARGES   ★ BRONTES   ★ STEROPES

★ CYCLOPES

★ god
✤ goddess
✹ man
✣ woman

CYCLOPES

*Gigantic one-eyed monsters;
their name means "circle-eye."*

There are two different traditions about the Cyclopes. In one, they were lawless pastoralists, residing in the Phlegraean Fields near Naples, whom Odysseus encountered on his travels (see Polyphemus). In the other tradition, Uranus (sky) and Gaia (earth) produced, among other children, three giants with one eye in the middle of the forehead: Arges (Bright), Brontes (Thunderer), and Steropes (Lightning-maker).

Uranus imprisoned these three giants because he feared they would depose him. Some believed he hid them in Tartarus, the abyss of the Underworld; others said he sent them to live in Mount Etna, where their terrible roars caused volcanic eruptions. In both traditions, Gaia plotted to avenge the act with the aid of one of her other children, Cronus. Uranus was overthrown and Cronus released the Cyclopes for a period of time, but when he felt threatened, he cast them back into Tartarus.

When Cronus was overthrown by his youngest son Zeus in the ten-year Titanomachy (war of the Titans), the Cyclopes were freed. In gratitude, they became Zeus' servants and the makers of his thunderbolts. They also made wonderful objects for his brothers: a trident for Poseidon and the cap of invisibility for his son Perseus. For the huntress Artemis, they made a silver bow and a quiver of arrows. In return, she gave them the bodies of her prey to devour.

The Cyclopes were skilled workers. They were credited by the Greeks with building the massive fortifications at Tiryns and Mycenae in the Peloponnese. The Romans believed that the Cyclopes worked as smiths in Vulcan's forge at Mount Etna.

ONE-EYED GIANTS
*A Gallo-Roman funerary mask
depicting one of the
Cyclopes. The single
eye in the middle
of the forehead
is clearly
visible.*

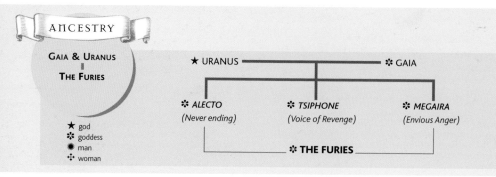

ANCESTRY

GAIA & URANUS
|
THE FURIES

★ god
❊ goddess
✳ man
✢ woman

★ URANUS ———————————— ✣ GAIA

❊ ALECTO   ✣ TSIPHONE   ✣ MEGAIRA
(Never ending)   (Voice of Revenge)   (Envious Anger)

✣ THE FURIES

THE FURIES

Three female avengers of wrong. In particular, they pursued relentlessly those who were guilty of murder within a family or clan.

The Furies were known as *Erinyes* in ancient Greek, meaning "the angry ones." They were said to have been born from the blood of Uranus that fell upon Gaia after his castration by Cronus.

The primeval birth of the Furies set them apart from other immortals. Even their names have an implacable ring: Alecto (Never-ending), Tsiphone (Voice of Revenge), and Megaira (Envious Anger). The Furies were hags, entwined with snakes, brandishing torches and whips, and were looked upon as pitiless pursuers of the guilty. The effect of the Furies on their victims was to drive them mad. Their powers were so great that the ancient Greeks never dared to mention them by name. When not hounding the guilty on earth, the three avengers tortured wrongdoers in the Underworld.

AVENGING MURDER

When Orestes murdered his mother Clytemnestra in revenge for her part in the killing of his father Agamemnon, King of Mycenae, the Furies pursued him relentlessly. Despite the support of Orestes' act from the god of prophecy, Apollo, the Furies were determined to avenge the matricide. At Apollo's shrine at Delphi, they demanded blood for blood. They were persuaded to stay their hand only by the gods, who declared that the case should be referred to the ancient Athenian court of the Areopagus. There, Athena, protectress of the city of Athens, ensured that Orestes was acquitted, but only on condition that he fulfilled a difficult task as punishment. Afterward, the Furies were known as the Eumenides ("the soothed ones").

FURIES BEFORE
GATES OF DIS
*A 17th-century
engraving depicting
a scene from Dante's
Inferno, showing
the furies as
snake-entwined,
winged hags.*

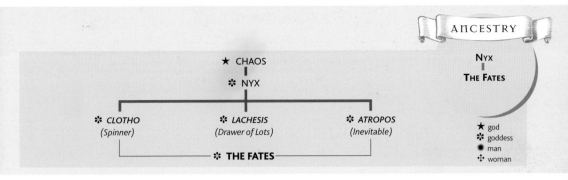

★ CHAOS
|
❋ NYX

❋ CLOTHO
(Spinner)

❋ LACHESIS
(Drawer of Lots)

❋ ATROPOS
(Inevitable)

❋ THE FATES

★ god
❋ goddess
✷ man
✤ woman

THE FATES

Three goddesses, known as the Moirai ("allotters"), who decided the individual fates of the ancient Greeks.

The three Fates were Clotho (Spinner), Lachesis (Drawer of Lots), and Atropos (Inevitable). As the daughters of Nyx (Night), the Fates may have developed from a group of birth spirits, deities concerned with supervising the future lives of babies. Their original purpose may have been to determine the fate of each individual at birth.

Gradually, the Fates acquired a wider role in mythology, although the power of their decrees was not always clear. For example, was Zeus, the king of gods and men, subject to them, or could he alter what the Fates decreed? Sometimes, Zeus appeared to be superior, but he was probably best known as the hand of destiny rather than the power that decided its course.

OLD WEAVERS

The Fates were envisaged as three old women, spinning men's fate like thread. Clotho spun destinies on her spindle, Lachesis measured length with a rod, and Atropos cut them with shears. When the Fates had arranged the time of death, the malevolent Ceres appeared. These female spirits, with pointed claws and bloodstained cloaks, delivered the fatal blow and took their victims to the land of shadows.

Men often arrogantly thought they could control their destiny by leading risk-free lives. Some gods even mocked the Fates—Apollo once tricked them into getting drunk so that he could prevent a friend's death. At the oracular shrine at Delphi only two Fates were revered—Birth and Death. It was believed that when Zeus claimed sovereignty over the Fates, he assumed the measuring role of Lachesis. .

GOYA'S BLACK PAINTINGS *This fresco in Goya's own home shows the Fates at work, with Clotho spinning and Lachesis holding up a lorgnette (eyeglasses with a short handle).*

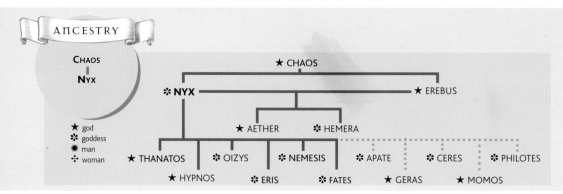

Chaos
|
Nyx

★ CHAOS

❋ NYX ———————————————— ★ EREBUS

★ AETHER   ❋ HEMERA

★ god
❋ goddess
✳ man
✢ woman

★ THANATOS   ❋ OIZYS   ❋ NEMESIS   ❋ APATE   ❋ CERES   ❋ PHILOTES

★ HYPNOS   ❋ ERIS   ❋ FATES   ★ GERAS   ★ MOMOS

NYX

Goddess of the night.

Nyx was considered to be among the first deities ever to exist, having emerged from Chaos. With her brother Erebus, Nyx gave birth to Aether (Atmosphere) and Hemera (Day), but later, on her own, she produced a number of other children. In some legends, she also gave birth to Apate (Deceit), Geras (Old Age), Ceres (Doom), Momos (Blame), and Philotes (Tenderness), most of whom resided in the Underworld.

In several ancient Greek texts, Nyx appears as the first principle, even before Chaos. The poems attributed to Orpheus (known as the Orphics) describe Nyx as a goddess with awesome black wings who lived in the Underworld by day and only came out at dusk. She was courted by the Wind and laid a

NYX, GODDESS OF THE NIGHT
Night is identified by the mask under her left shoulder and the owl that peers out from under her raised left leg.

silver egg in the womb of Darkness. In Orphic legends, Night is regarded as having prophetic power, an attribute of Gaia.

In Homer's Iliad, "all-subduing" Night is the only deity that Zeus fears. During one of Heracles' labors, Hypnos (Sleep) lulled Zeus into drowsiness, during which time a storm arose. Zeus, the god of weather, woke up and was enraged to see that Heracles had been driven off course. The god threatened to punish Hypnos by casting him into the dark abyss of Erebus. However, when Hypnos fled into the arms of Nyx, Zeus was

forced to retract his threat because he dared not cross the mighty goddess of the night.

NIGHT WORSHIP
Night was a feature of some cults of ancient Greece and Asia Minor (present-day Turkey). A statue of Night was displayed in the Temple of Artemis at Ephesus. The Spartans had a cult of Sleep and Death who were twins, and believed to be the offspring of Nyx.

ERIS

Goddess of strife and quarrel.

ANCESTRY

❋ NYX

❋ ERIS

NYX
|
ERIS

★ god
❋ goddess
✳ man
✢ woman

Eris was the troublesome daughter of Nyx (Night). Although she was not invited to the wedding of Peleus and Thetis, parents of Achilles, she went nevertheless and threw a golden apple through the door bearing the inscription: "For the fairest." This caused an argument among the three beautiful goddesses present: Hera, Athena, and Aphrodite. Zeus sent the beauties to Mount Ida near Troy to be judged by the prince Paris. He chose Aphrodite as the greatest beauty, and she in turn gave Paris Helen's hand in marriage.

In some traditions, Eris was known as the sister of Ares (god of war), who helped him foster battles; she reveled in the anguish and bloodiness of war. She filled their hearts with animosity in the hope that they would fight to the death, as did Atreus and Thyestes, sons of Pelops. Not surprisingly, no one loved this cruel deity, who is usually depicted in art as an ugly harridan with an unquenchable thirst for discord.

Eris' ways of inveigling men into her possession were subtle, for she did not say to them, "Behold my face and my shape," for that would have disgusted them. Instead, she played on their insecurities, inflated their pride, and suggested their superiority over their neighbors. She conceptualized the tensions between men and women in numerous ways. Many became obsessed by her and were punished for their foolishness.

No wonder the ancient Greek dramatist Euripides, who wrote tragedies about human passions and social issues, declared, "Truly, Eris is a goddess to fear."

As well as creating rivalry and jealousy between people, Eris produced disharmony within a person's being. An unhealthy body or disease was considered a clear indication that someone had been afflicted by Eris, and it was believed that strife could cause imbalance in the mind, such as madness or depression, or simply unhappiness.

THE JUDGEMENT OF PARIS
Eris (top, with black wings) throws the golden apple into the gathering of guests at the wedding of Thetis and Peleus.

NEMESIS

Goddess of retribution.

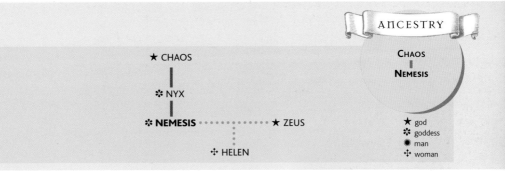

★ CHAOS

❄ NYX

❄ NEMESIS · · · · · · · · · · · · ★ ZEUS

⁘ HELEN

CHAOS
|
NEMESIS

★ god
❄ goddess
✹ man
⁘ woman

Nemesis, agent of vengeance, embodied the gods' anger. Above all, she was associated with punishing mortals who succumbed to hubris or pride. For example, she pursued Agamemnon for showing excessive pride in the Greeks' victory over the Trojans.

The word in common use today means "just retribution," or "just deserts," but originally Nemesis was known simply as the dispenser of fortune, with no subtext of punishment or reward. In time, Nemesis acquired the additional function of rectifying the balance of justice and taking account of the resentment caused by the disturbance of this balance.

In one legend, Zeus lusted after Nemesis, who had some of Aphrodite's beauty, and he pursued her around the world. To evade his clutches, she constantly changed shape. On one occasion she turned herself into a goose, prompting Zeus to disguise himself as a swan, and he was successful in catching and then violating her. Helen of Troy was hatched from the egg she laid. Some say that Nemesis was Helen's mother and that Leda, wife of the King of Sparta, suckled and reared the child. It is thought that this story may have been composed as a justification for the catastrophe of the Trojan War. Later, Greeks identified Nemesis with Adrastea, the "Inescapable One," which is close in idea to her sisters, the Fates.

IN ART

Nemesis had a fiery aspect and was commonly depicted with a balance in one hand and a whip or an axe in the other. The German artist Albrecht Dürer painted a curious image of Nemesis as a winged female floating in the clouds above a rural landscape, balanced on a small globe. Themes of temperance and restraint from temptation are mixed with uncertainty.

FORTUNA

The Roman counterpart to Nemesis was Fortuna, which means "she who turns the year about." In some ways, Fortuna is closer to the original understanding of Nemesis as a pastoral nymph-goddess who held sway over seasonal fortunes. Her symbol was the wheel, whose spokes represented seasonal changes. In Roman times, this goddess came to be associated with chance. That she showed no respect for class in her distribution of fortune is evident in her festival, held every June, in which slaves were allowed to participate.

During the Middle Ages, the idea of Fortune's wheel was a powerful concept. In Malory's *Morte d'Arthur*, printed in 1485, there is a graphic description of the wheel which appeared to Arthur in a dream, just before his fateful battle against Modred.

DIVINE RETRIBUTION
A 2nd- or 3rd-century AD Roman relief from Lattaquié, Syria, showing Nemesis with weighing scales. The scales refer to her role in restoring the balance of justice.

CRONUS/
SATURN

*Youngest son of Gaia
(Earth) and Uranus (Sky).*

The Titans (giants) were the cleverest offspring of Gaia and her son Uranus, the first divine pair. All Uranus' children were imprisoned in Gaia's body. To end this uncomfortable situation, Gaia gave Cronus, her youngest son, a flint sickle and the next time that the couple mated, Cronus attacked Uranus, castrating him. Thereby, Cronus seized control of the world.

When Cronus threw down his father's severed genitals, the drops of blood became the Furies, giants and nymphs. In another version of the tale, Cronus flung the genitals into the sea, where foam gathered around them and produced the love goddess Aphrodite.

Cronus' reign soon became as tyrannical as that of his father. He forced the giants, including the Cyclopes, underground and swallowed his children at birth whenever his wife Rhea delivered them, because he had been

SATURN DEVOURING CHILD
This painting (left), by Rubens, captures some of the horror of the myth in which Cronus (Saturn) resorted to eating his children in order to prevent them from usurping him.

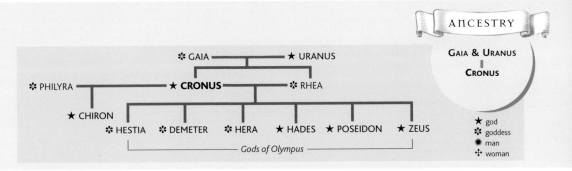

✤ GAIA ———— ★ URANUS

✤ PHILYRA ———— ★ **CRONUS** ———— ✤ RHEA

★ CHIRON

✤ HESTIA ✤ DEMETER ✤ HERA ★ HADES ★ POSEIDON ★ ZEUS

Gods of Olympus

★ god
✤ goddess
✵ man
✤ woman

warned by Gaia that he would be deposed by one of his offspring. Rhea managed to save the last of her six children, Zeus, whom she smuggled with Gaia's help to the island of Crete as soon as he was born. Here he was hidden in a cave and cared for by the nymphs. In time, Zeus took revenge on his father and, with the aid of the Titans, flung him into the abyss of Tartarus, where giants with a hundred arms

guarded him. In another version of the myth, Cronus was exiled to an island near Britain where he slept with his followers.

A GOLDEN AGE BEFORE THE GREEKS

According to the tradition of Hesiod, dating back to 700 BC, the first men alive were contemporaries of Cronus and lived in a Golden Age, free from worry and fatigue. In fact,

Cronus had been worshiped as a god before the Greeks settled in their land. He was probably deposed, therefore, to allow Zeus and the gods of Mount Olympus to rise to prominence.

SATURN, BENEVOLENT ROMAN GOD

Like Cronus, this ancient Italian god of agriculture was regarded as the ruler of a distant Golden Age, when life was easy and peaceful. During this age he had taught people how to till the fields and enjoy a civilized way of life.

As early as the fifth century BC Saturn's temple stood in the Forum at Rome and acted as the treasury. His festival, the Saturnalia, took place in December and lasted seven days. During the revels, people ate together and exchanged gifts at a public banquet in the Forum. At this time slaves were also temporarily given their liberty.

As an agricultural deity, Saturn has more in common with a Greek goddess of agriculture, such as Demeter, than with Cronus. His name may have derived from the Latin *satus*, meaning "sown." The Romans believed that Saturn arrived in Italy from Greece, where Jupiter had threatened to harm him. This is obviously an echo of the quarrel between Cronus and his son Zeus.

The planet Saturn is named after the god, as is Saturday.

4th-century stele dedicated to Saturn. The sheep indicates the pastoral associations of the Roman god.

THE GODS OF

OLYMPUS

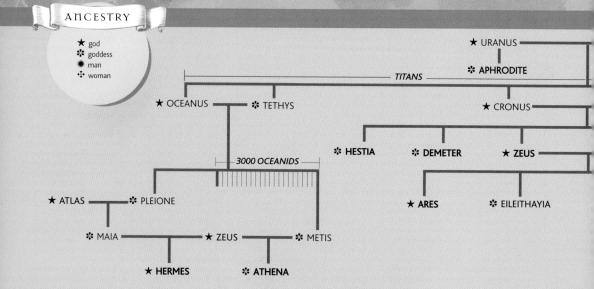

ANCESTRY

- ★ god
- ❋ goddess
- ✹ man
- ✤ woman

★ URANUS

❋ APHRODITE

TITANS

★ OCEANUS ── ❋ TETHYS

★ CRONUS

❋ HESTIA   ❋ DEMETER   ★ ZEUS

3000 OCEANIDS

★ ATLAS ── ❋ PLEIONE

★ ARES   ❋ EILEITHAYIA

❋ MAIA ── ★ ZEUS ── ❋ METIS

★ HERMES   ❋ ATHENA

In Greek and Roman mythology the twelve gods of Olympus, eleven of whom were descended from Cronus, ruled the world after the defeat of the Titans. Most were believed to dwell on Mount Olympus, the highest mountain in Greece (at nearly 10,000 feet), whose peaks were shrouded in cloud and therefore hidden from mortal sight. Olympus was presided over by Zeus and his wife Hera. With them lived Zeus' brother Poseidon and their sisters Demeter and Hestia. Hades, the other brother of Zeus and ruler of the Underworld, rarely visited Olympus and so was not regarded as an Olympian god. With six of Zeus' children, these comprised the twelve Olympian gods.

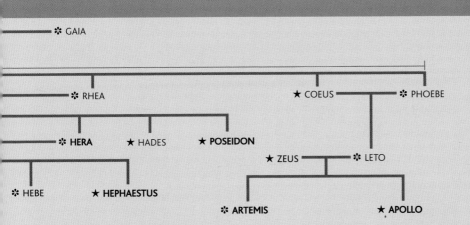

ZEUS/JUPITER

Known as god of the weather, Zeus was king of the gods in Greek mythology. In Roman mythology he was known as Jupiter.

Zeus, supreme ruler of the gods, hurled down mighty thunderbolts on all who opposed his will. His domain was the storm, with its lightning, thunder, snow, and hail.

Zeus' mother Rhea saved him from the fate suffered by his siblings: being swallowed by their father Cronus. He was taken as a baby to the island of Crete where he was brought up secretly by the nymphs. When he reached manhood, Zeus forced his father to vomit up his swallowed brothers and sisters. The siblings then rebelled against Cronus and his giant relations, the Titans, in a great struggle known as the Titanomachy, which lasted for ten years. The offspring of Cronus became known as the gods of Olympus, because they lived on Mount Olympus, while the Titans based themselves on Mount Othrys. During the Titanomachy, Zeus called on the Cyclopes (who forged his thunderbolts), and three giants with a hundred arms, whom he brought up from the dreaded abyss of Tartarus. In an awesome barrage of thunder, lightning, rocks, and flames, the Titans were defeated. Zeus condemned Cronus and the Titans who supported him to eternal torment in the depths of Tartarus, where the hundred-armed giants guarded them.

THE CHALLENGE OF TYPHON

After defeating the Titans, Zeus faced another challenge, in the form of a terrifying monster

---

ZEUS AND SEMELE
Jealous Hera tricked the mortal, pregnant Semele into making Zeus appear in his godly form. Mortals cannot look upon gods without dying. See Dionysus, pages 70–71.

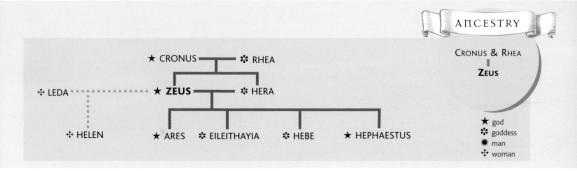

ANCESTRY

★ CRONUS ── ❋ RHEA

❖ LEDA .... ★ **ZEUS** ── ❋ HERA

❖ HELEN ★ ARES ❋ EILEITHAYIA ❖ HEBE ★ HEPHAESTUS

CRONUS & RHEA
|
ZEUS

★ god
❋ goddess
✳ man
❖ woman

called Typhon. This creature, born of Gaia (Earth), was endowed with a snake's tail and a hundred heads bearing fiery eyes, dark tongues, and voices like thunder. As soon as Typhon emerged from the cave of his birthplace, Zeus attacked him with a hail of thunderbolts. Undeterrred by the onslaught, a fierce battle took place, during which the monster grabbed Zeus and tore out the sinews from his limbs, leaving the god lying helpless on the ground.

Fortunately, the cunning Hermes discovered where the missing sinews were hidden, recovered them, and fed them back into Zeus' limbs. Zeus, fit again, renewed his attacks on Typhon and eventually was victorious by picking up an island from the sea off Italy (now known as Sicily) to crush the monster. Typhon, however, was immortal and so could never die. His fiery breath can still be seen issuing from Mount Etna.

LORDS OF THE WORLD
When the Titanic struggles finally came to an end, Zeus and his brothers, Poseidon and Hades, divided the world between them, drawing lots for three different realms: Zeus became lord of the sky, Poseidon of the sea, and Hades of the Underworld; the earth was regarded as common territory.

Zeus married Hera but had many consorts, both human and divine. For his encounters with mortal women, he appeared in various guises, famously that of a swan in order to seduce Leda, from whose union Helen of Troy was born. As king of the gods, Zeus influenced destiny, although control over it lay with the Fates.

LEDA AND THE SWAN
Zeus often took the form of other creatures in order to pursue mortal women. Here, he is shown as a swan, in which guise he and Leda begat Polydeuces and Helen of Troy. See pages 89 and 126–127 for more.

JUPITER

Also known as Jove, Jupiter was the Romans' chief god, called Optimum Maximus ("the Great and Good"). From earliest times he was the protector of vineyards and the harvest. As Rome developed into a city, Jupiter gradually lost his agricultural associations and became god of the city and eventually controlled all human affairs.

Jupiter's wife was Juno (identified with the Greek goddess Hera). Their relations were less troubled than those of Hera and Zeus, although Juno was angered by the birth of Minerva from Jupiter's head without the help of a mother. Helped by the goddess Flora, she bore the war god Mars without having sexual relations. This belligerent son rivaled Jupiter for the affections of the warlike Romans.

HERA / JUNO

Sister and wife of Zeus, and queen of heaven; principally a mother goddess. The Roman equivalent was Juno.

This daughter of Cronus and Rhea was swallowed at birth by her father, who feared that his children would overthrow him. When Zeus forced their father to yield her up, the king of the gods decided that Hera should be his wife. Hera had four children by Zeus: the war god Ares, the smith god Hephaestus, the goddess of childbirth Ilithyia, and Hebe, the cup-bearer of the gods. When the goddess Athena emerged from Zeus' head, Hera was so furious at Zeus' adultery that, in one story, she immediately gave birth to the monster Typhon. (Typhon, however, is usually known as Gaia's child.)

Hera was a jealous goddess who persecuted the children Zeus had with other goddesses and mortal women. In fact, the quarrels of Zeus and Hera were often so fierce that they shook Mount Olympus, the gods' home. Once, Zeus was so angry about Hera's mistreatment of the hero Heracles that he suspended her by her wrists from a pinnacle of Mount Olympus and hung weights on her feet.

SEXUAL PLEASURE

Perhaps the fiercest argument between Hera and Zeus concerned sexual love. Hera insisted that the male received most pleasure, while Zeus believed it was the opposite. Their argument raged, so they agreed to consult Tiresias, who had been both man and woman. His declaration that a woman has nine times as much sexual pleasure as a man so infuriated Hera that she blinded him. By way of compensation, Zeus gave Tiresias the gift of prophecy.

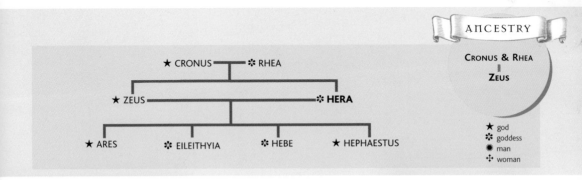

ANCESTRY

CRONUS & RHEA

ZEUS

★ CRONUS ——— ❄ RHEA

★ ZEUS ——————————————— ❄ **HERA**

★ ARES   ❄ EILEITHYIA   ❄ HEBE   ★ HEPHAESTUS

★ god
❄ goddess
✳ man
✥ woman

JUNO

Wife to Jupiter and closely connected with fertility, Juno probably originated as an early Italian moon goddess. The counterpart story to that of the Greek trio of Athena, Zeus, and Hera involves Minerva springing from Jupiter's head. This adultery so infuriated Juno that she complained to the goddess Flora, who was responsible for making plants produce flowers. At the touch of a magic herb provided by Flora, Juno became pregnant and gave birth to Mars, god of war, just as in Greek mythology Hera bore Ares.

As the genesis of womanhood, Juno ensured the continuity of the family. The month of June, once called Junonius, was considered to be the most favorable month for weddings.

ECHO AND NARCISSUS

In Greek mythology, a mountain nymph named Echo chattered to Hera ceaselessly in order to distract her attention from the adulterous behavior of her husband Zeus. Hera found the chatter so irritating that she removed Echo's power of speech, leaving her capable of only repeating what others said.

Another version of the story says that Echo wasted away to an echoing voice when the beautiful youth Narcissus spurned her offer of love. In punishment for his aloofness, the gods made him fall in love with his own image, reflected in a pool of water. Unable to possess the image, he pined away until he died (possibly by suicide), when he was changed into a flower, the narcissus.

THE BIRTH OF THE MILKY WAY WITH HERCULES AND JUNO
Rubens' painting beautifully depicts how Hercules became immortal by being suckled by Juno

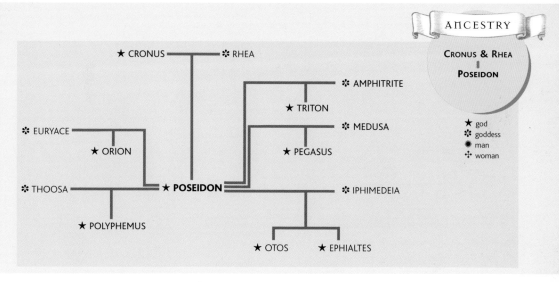

★ god
❋ goddess
✳ man
✢ woman

POSEIDON/NEPTUNE

Poseidon was the Greek god of the seas and water; Neptune was the Roman equivalent.

Cronus had three sons— Zeus, Hades, and Poseidon—who overthrew their father and divided the world between them. Poseidon became the ruler of the sea, a role he performed with considerable violence. The sea god's rages were terrifying, especially when he stirred up the waves with his magic trident, a gift from the Cyclopes. Poseidon also caused earthquakes. He lived beneath the Aegean Sea in a palace, from which he rode out in a chariot pulled by majestic seahorses. On one occasion, Poseidon dared to challenge Zeus' supremacy. With the aid of the goddesses Hera and Athena,

Poseidon planned to bind up Zeus, but was thwarted by the hundred-armed monster Brareus, whom Zeus summoned from Tartarus for his protection.

Most of Poseidon's children inherited their father's violent temperament. His son Polyphemus, a Cyclopes, was notorious for eating some of Odysseus' followers. The Greek leader managed to escape only by blinding Polyphemus with the heated end of a stake, an injury for which Poseidon found it hard to forgive Odysseus.

ENEMY OF THE TROJANS
In the works of the epic poet Homer, Poseidon is the implacable foe of the Trojans.

This hostility arose from the dishonesty of the Trojan king, Laomendon, father of Priam. The king had agreed to give Apollo and Poseidon a sum of money for building the walls of Troy, but, when the task was completed, he refused to pay them. Although Apollo was content to send a plague on the Trojans in punishment, Poseidon was not satisfied until Troy had been sacked by the Greeks.

Neptune, Poseidon's Roman counterpart, was a less important god, probably because the sea was not as significant to the Romans as it was to the Greeks.

NEPTUNE ON A HORSE
A 17th-century painting depicting Poseidon riding through the seas on a horse. He is holding the trident made for him by the Cyclopes.

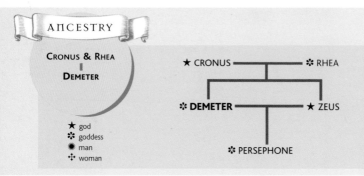

CRONUS & RHEA

DEMETER

★ CRONUS ——— ✳ RHEA

✳ DEMETER ——— ★ ZEUS

✳ PERSEPHONE

★ god
✳ goddess
✴ man
✣ woman

DEMETER / CERES

Earth goddess in ancient Greece, specifically the goddess of vegetation and fruitfulness of the land. Her equivalent in Roman mythology was Ceres.

Demeter means "mother earth" and she was sometimes identified with Gaia (Earth). Her cultic myths explain the annual cycle of the seasons, the growth and withering of vegetation, the inconsistency of harvests, and the difference between summer and winter. Her main influence was over corn, the staple food of the Greeks.

Demeter was a devoted, caring mother, and the most important story in her mythology concerns her relationship with her daughter. Demeter was especially close to her brother Zeus (incestuous relationships among the gods of Olympus were acceptable), and their union produced Persephone. When their daughter was still very young, and without consulting Demeter, Zeus agreed that Hades, king of the Underworld, could marry her. Some years later, while Persephone was picking flowers in a meadow with the daughter

of Oceanus, the ground split apart as she bent down to pick a narcissus. Hades rode up in his chariot drawn by dark blue steeds and kidnapped her.

Demeter was inconsolable when she discovered that her daughter had vanished, and with two burning torches began searching the earth for her. She refused to eat or wash, as did Persephone, who was pining away in Hades' gloomy kingdom.

When all looked hopeless, Demeter met the earth goddess Hecate who knew about Persephone's abduction. She took Demeter to the sun god Helius, who told her that Persephone had in fact married Hades and was queen of a vast realm. In her despair, Demeter sent a famine across the Earth lasting a year and threatened to destroy manind. To placate her, Zeus sent Hermes to fetch her beloved daughter from Hades, but before Persephone departed, Hades gave

DEMETER, EARTH GODDESS
A marble copy of a 4th century BC original.

her some pomegranate seeds to bind her to his realm. From then on, Persephone returned to the earth each year in spring, like the corn itself, but she always went back to Hades at the beginning of winter.

There are similar legends about the Roman goddess Ceres, including stories of how she wandered through the world distributing grain and advising men how to grow it. The word "cereal" derives from her name.

ANCESTRY

CRONUS & RHEA
|
HESTIA

★ CRONUS ——————— ✺ RHEA

✺ **HESTIA**

★ god
✺ goddess
✳ man
✣ woman

HESTIA/ VESTA

In Greek mythology Hestia was the goddess of the hearth and the home; her Roman equivalent was Vesta.

Hestia swore on Zeus' head to remain a virgin for all time, even declining offers of marriage from both Poseidon and Apollo. Her fidelity to the vow of chastity is confirmed by the absence of any revealing tales about her, which in itself is hardly surprising, since she never left home. By resisting all amorous advances, Hestia preserved the peace of the gods' homestead at Olympus. On one occasion at an outdoor feast, when all the gods present had fallen asleep, Priapus, in a drunken state, tried to violate her. Fortunately, an ass brayed and Hestia woke up to find Priapus about to invade her, whereupon she screamed so loudly that he departed in fright.

Normally, Hestia was calm and charitable; as the goddess of the hearth, householders everywhere called on her for protection. The home fire was sacred to the goddess, and the hearth was the center of life for the ancient Greeks, who would not hold a banquet without first offering sacrifices to her. Misfortune would befall anyone who tried to violate a person under Hestia's protection.

VESTA

In Rome, the shrine of Vesta featured an eternal flame, in which Vesta was believed to exist. The temple was guarded by six Vestal Virgins. Like the moral imperative adopted by Hestia in Greek mythology, the Vestal Virgins had to remain pure; any

GODDESS OF HEARTH AND HOME
The most gentle, peace-loving, and charitable of the Olympian gods, Hestia never left Mount Olympus. Though she was a popular goddess, she was rarely depicted in ancient art. This detail of Hestia is from an Athenian red-figure clay vase c.500 BC.

lapses were punished severely, which usually meant being buried alive. One of the priestesses, Rhea Silvia, was raped by the war god Mars and gave birth to twins, Romulus (founder of Rome) and Remus.

ARES/MARS

God of war in Greek and Roman mythology, respectively.

A res had no wife, and perhaps for this reason he constantly fell under the spell of Aphrodite, goddess of love. They produced four children out of wedlock in a scandalous liaison that was ended by Zeus.

Another child of Ares, a daughter born of a mortal woman, was raped on the slopes of the Acropolis in Athens by one of the sea god Poseidon's sons, Halirrhothius. When the enraged Ares exacted retribution by murdering the rapist, Poseidon brought the war god to trial in Athens. Ares was acquitted and later the court became known as Areopagus (Hill of Ares).

An unpopular god, Ares was not generally worshiped by the Greeks, who were afraid of his lust for violence and cruelty. Such a vicious deity was not considered trustworthy, so Ares did not receive the reverence shown by the Romans to Mars.

MARS

Along with Jupiter, Mars was the favorite god of the Romans. His month, March, was very important in society because it heralded the rebirth of plant life and the new season of wars and campaigns. Originally, Mars was identified with a pastoral deity, Silvanus; even after he became the great war god, Mars retained something of this association with the earth.

Mars was conceived out of spite by Juno, because her husband Jupiter had produced Minerva without her aid. As revenge, Juno enlisted the help of Flora, goddess of flowering, who

MARS, GOD OF WAR
An imposing marble bust of the god wearing full military regalia.

touched Juno with a magical herb, which in turn brought about the birth of Mars.

Mars fathered the founder of Rome, Romulus, and was forever invoked on the battlefield to strengthen the resolve of Roman soldiers.

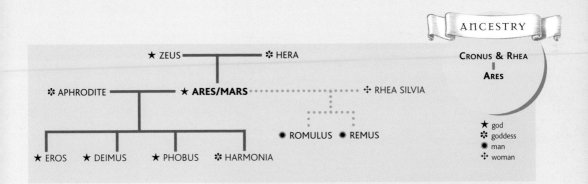

ANCESTRY

ZEUS ━━━ HERA

APHRODITE ━━━ ARES/MARS ·········· RHEA SILVIA

EROS ★ DEIMUS ★ PHOBUS ✤ HARMONIA

ROMULUS ✹ REMUS

CRONUS & RHEA
ARES

★ god
✤ goddess
✹ man
✣ woman

APHRODITE & ARES' ADULTERY
A 17th-century English tapestry illustrating the story of Hephaestus trapping his wife, Aphrodite, in bed with Ares. Hephaestus trapped the adulterous lovers in a net he had made himself from the lightest steel. Poseidon, shown with his trident, eventually convinced Hephaestus to let the lovers go in exchange for a fine. This is the story as told by Homer in the Odyssey.

ROMULUS AND REMUS

Romulus was perhaps the greatest gift Mars gave to the Romans, although ill-conceived. Mars was said to have raped Rhea Silvia, a Vestal Virgin, while she drew water from a spring in his sacred grove, and the result was the birth of twin sons, Romulus and Remus. As priestesses sworn to chastity, it was a cardinal sin for a Vestal Virgin to lose her virginity, so when it became known that Rhea Silvia had given birth to twins, she was condemned as a fallen priestess and imprisoned. Luckily, years later her sons rescued her from captivity, and Romulus founded the city of Rome soon afterwards.

ATHENA/MINERVA

Virgin goddess of war and wisdom, and patroness of the arts and crafts; her Roman equivalent was known as Minerva.

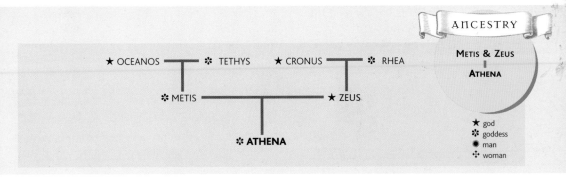

★ OCEANOS — ❋ TETHYS   ★ CRONUS — ❋ RHEA

❋ METIS — ★ ZEUS

❋ ATHENA

METIS & ZEUS

ATHENA

★ god
❋ goddess
✴ man
✢ woman

The Greek goddess Athena sprang into being when the smith god Hephaestus released her, fully formed and armed, from Zeus' head by splitting it open with an axe. There are different accounts of the legend of Athena's birth, but common to all was Zeus' fear of the future power of his child, about which he had been forewarned. Zeus' bid to rid himself of the fetus took the form of tricking Metis, his first wife and mother of the unborn child, into changing into a fly, which he then swallowed.

Another account of the story tells how Zeus did not wish to follow in the footsteps of his father Cronus, who swallowed most of his children. Unable to bring himself to eat the newborn Athena, Zeus swallowed Metis instead while she was still pregnant. It was also said that Zeus desired what Metis (meaning "thought" or "counsel") possessed—namely, her knowledge—and for that reason he pursued her avidly. Metis, however, was concerned to preserve her virginity and, in an

attempt to do so, changed herself into a fly, but Zeus caught her. In all versions of the story, Metis gave birth to Athena in his head.

PROTECTRESS OF ATHENS

From earliest times, Athena was connected with citadels. During the chaotic period after the fall of the Myceneans (*c.*1100 BCE), only the stronghold of Athens, the Acropolis, was able to withstand the onslaught. Not surprisingly, then, Athena was adopted as the protectress of the city. When Athens later developed into a commercial center, the Greeks believed that Athena protected its craftsmen, the source of the city's wealth, and so she became the patroness of the arts and crafts.

LUST, JEALOUSY, AND THE SERPENT KING

Athens already had a smith god, Hephaestus, who tried several times to seduce Athena. During one struggle his semen fell to the ground, whereupon it became

the serpent-king Erichthonius. This was the closest Athena ever came to producing a son. She entrusted the young child to the three daughters of Cecrops, an early ruler who was said to be a snake himself. Under the princesses' care, the child was put in a covered box and Athena ordered them not to look inside. However, two of the girls could not resist, and peeked inside the box. When they set eyes on the serpent-child they became mad with fright and killed themselves. Athena took Erichthonius to her temple on the Acropolis and raised him there, and he was made king of the Athenians.

CULT OF MINERVA

Like Athena of Athens, Minerva became a protectress of Rome. Her cult grew at the expense of the Roman war god Mars. Just as Athena was born of Zeus' head, so Minerva issued from the head of Jupiter without the aid of his wife Juno, much to her chagrin.

PALLAS ATHENA
A late tradition says Athena adopted the name of her friend, Pallas, who was killed while sparring with Athena.

BOLD OWL

Athena's symbol was the owl, a creature associated with the boldness of wisdom. In a variety of situations she aided heroes and adventurers, including Perseus, Heracles, Jason, and Odysseus. She enjoyed the bravery and daring of men on the battlefield, and, though she had a bloodthirsty streak, tended not to indulge in senseless slaughter, unlike the war god Ares.

APOLLO

Twin brother of Artemis; god of music, poetry, prophecy, and medicine, and protector of herds and flocks.

According to one legend, just four days after his birth on the island of Delos in the Cyclades, Apollo determined to exact revenge on the serpent Python for molesting his mother during her pregnancy. Python, son of Gaia (Earth), was the guardian of the Oracle at Delphi, at the time in the hands of the Titaness Themis. The serpent's breath was said to issue from deep within a chasm and contained prophecies encoded in its fumes. At the temple, a priestess would inhale the fumes and utter the often puzzling Oracle, which took the form of a riddle. When Python tried to prevent Apollo from approaching the chasm, the god killed the beast and took possession of the Oracle. Apollo was said to have learned the art of divination from Pan and so was able to take over the role of protecting the oracle.

GOD OF LIGHT

The outcome of this myth represents a triumph for the Olympian gods of light over those of earthly darkness. Apollo was worshiped as the god of light. His high moral and intellectual status gave him first rank as a nurturer of civilization. After his inauguration at Delphi, Apollo became associated with music, medicine, and archery. This wide range of patronage led him into contact with various nymphs and female mortals, but despite having numerous sexual encounters, few resulted in long-term relationships.

One of Apollo's exploits involved the Spartan prince Hyacinthus. Apollo was not the only god with a keen eye on this beautiful youth. One day, while Apollo was teaching the boy the art of discus-throwing, Zephyrus (god of the West Wind) blew up and caught the discus in mid-air. In an act of jealousy, Zephyrus threw it against Hyacinthus' skull and killed him. His spilled blood produced the hyacinth flower.

IN ART

In the Middle Ages, Apollo was usually depicted as a scholar, and later he appeared in paintings alongside the Muses. Louis XIV used Apollo's symbol, the sun, as a personal emblem in his title, the Sun King. The Apollo Belvedere, a marble replica of a Hellenistic bronze found in

APOLLO'S CHARIOT
Apollo, riding through the sky with his glorious chariot and attendants. This image represents Apollo's status as a god of light.

ANCESTRY

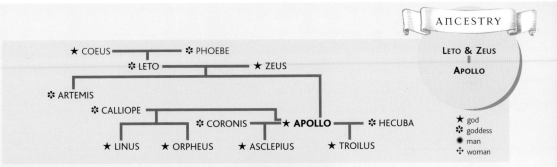

LETO & ZEUS
APOLLO

★ COEUS ──── ✤ PHOEBE
  ✤ LETO ──── ★ ZEUS
✤ ARTEMIS
  ✤ CALLIOPE
      ✤ CORONIS ── ★ **APOLLO** ── ✤ HECUBA
★ LINUS   ★ ORPHEUS   ★ ASCLEPIUS   ★ TROILUS

★ god
✤ goddess
✴ man
✣ woman

Rome, now stands in the Vatican Museum. Lord Byron, whose own features were compared to Apollo's, eulogized the form of this statue in his poem "Childe Harold's Pilgrimage." Stravinsky used the god as a character in his 1928 ballet *Apollo Musagetes*.

DAPHNE'S DISGUISE

Daphne was a mountain nymph from Thessaly who spurned men but was loved by both Apollo and the mortal Leucippus. Leucippus disguised himself as a nymph to woo her, but revealed his masculinity when bathing and was killed by the nymphs. Urged on by Eros, god of love, Apollo then began his pursuit of Daphne. In order to escape from him, she prayed to her father, the River Peneius, and he turned her into a laurel tree. To console himself, Apollo made a wreath from its leaves. The laurel tree became Apollo's cult symbol.

ARTEMIS/DIANA

*Goddess of the chase, the forest, and wild animals,
and twin sister of Apollo. The Roman equivalent
was Diana.*

Although born of uncertain parentage, Artemis and her twin brother Apollo are usually regarded as the result of a coupling between Zeus and the Titaness Leto. Consequently, the twins suffered persecution from Zeus' jealous wife Hera, who resented their births. One legend relates how, in revenge for Hera's animosity, Artemis helped Apollo fight and kill the serpent Python, who was said to belong to Hera.

Like her brother, Artemis was associated with death—she was responsible for the demise of women, while Apollo was responsible for the death of men. Her fierceness is obvious in several myths. For example, when her favorite follower, the nymph Callisto, bore Zeus a child, Artemis was so enraged by Callisto's lost virginity that she changed her into a bear and drove her away with arrows.

The giant hunter Orion was severely punished when, in one version of the story, he tried to rape Artemis. In revenge, she killed him with her arrows. But the fate of Actaeon, grandson of Apollo, was the most cruel of all.

During a hunt, this mortal had the misfortune of seeing Artemis bathing. The goddess considered herself so insulted that she turned Actaeon into a stag, and he was immediately devoured by his own hounds. Another version of the story says the young man was eaten alive as a rebuke for claiming to be a superior hunter to the goddess.

The harshness of Artemis, as well as her association with the wild, made her a dangerous goddess. She was therefore appeased with great care and received numerous animal sacrifices to win her favor.

DIANA

The Roman counterpart to Artemis was an ancient Italian goddess of the woodland. She was also goddess of the moon and the forests, and protector of women in childbirth. She was worshiped as a virgin goddess in her temple in Rome.

DIANA'S HUNT
*Diana and some of her many female
companions on a hunt. Her cult
involved the development of girls
into women.*

HECATE

A companion of Artemis on the hunt was the Titaness Hecate. Zeus and the Greeks treated her with great respect because she had unusual magical powers. Hecate was also known to be generous, bestowing wealth and good luck, as well as offering wise advice and guidance. However, if Hecate desired, she could use her powers in a sinister way, consorting with ghosts and practicing black magic (like Circe). In this guise she would appear entwined with snakes and hold the keys to the Underworld. In later mythology, Hecate became goddess of the moon, appearing as a deity with three heads—those of a lion, a horse, and a dog. During the Middle Ages, Diana and Hecate were regarded as leaders of the witches.

ANCESTRY

★ COEUS ——— ❁ PHOEBE

❁ LETO ——— ★ ZEUS

❁ **ARTEMIS** ★ APOLLO

LETO & ZEUS
ARTEMIS

★ god
❁ goddess
❁ man
❁ woman

APHRODITE/VENUS

Aphrodite, Greek goddess of love, beauty, and fertility; she was later identified with the Roman goddess Venus.

Aphrodite's name derives from the Greek for "foam" (aphros), which may refer to her birth at sea. She was formed, fully grown, into a beautiful goddess from the foam that floated around the castrated genitals of Uranus.

Although she was married to the lame smith god Hephaestus, Aphrodite seduced Ares, god of war, and had four children by him—Deimus (Fear), Phobus (Panic), Eros (Love), and a daughter Harmonia (Harmony). Suspecting the illicit liaison, Hephaestus successfully trapped Aphrodite and Ares in bed together by means of an invisible net. The other Olympian gods who witnessed the capture fell about laughing instead of sympathizing with Hephaestus' shame. Zeus, the arranger of Aphrodite's marriage to Hephaestus, was both disgusted at her behavior and attracted to her. Out of spite, he made her fall in love with a mortal, the Trojan Anchises, and bear him a son, the hero Aeneas.

So powerful a goddess was Aphrodite that she, in turn, was able to take revenge on Zeus. With unashamed glee, she made him chase after nymphs and mortal women, and neglect his wife Hera. Stories of the intense rivalry between Hera and Aphrodite recur often in Greek mythology, but the most important of these myths relates to the Judgment of Paris, which was the cause of the Trojan War. Paris, a Trojan prince and most handsome of men, was asked to choose "the fairest" beauty to be rewarded with the golden apple. Of the three goddesses presented to him—Hera, Athena, and Aphrodite—he preferred Aphrodite's offer of the love of the most beautiful woman in the world, and he gave her the prize. She rewarded him with the beautiful Helen, wife of the Spartan king Menelaus, an action that indirectly caused the Trojan War.

IN ART

The statue of Venus on the Capitoline Hill in Rome is one of the best-known statues of the goddess from antiquity. Another famous marble statue based on it is the *Venus de Milo* (named after the island of Melos where it was found), now in the Louvre in Paris. Rubens' *Venus Frigida* shows the goddess crouching by her bath in less confident mode, depicting the proverb, "Hunger and thirst cool love's ardour."

THE BIRTH OF VENUS
In Botticelli's painting, the Zephyrs, as symbols of spiritual passions, blow Venus inshore, where she is cloaked by a goddess of the seasons.

★ URANUS

★ ARES ──── ❋ **APHRODITE** ══ ━━━ ★ HEPHAESTUS

★ ANCHISES

★ AENEAS

★ EROS   ★ DEIMUS   ★ PHOBUS   ❋ HARMONIA

★ god
❋ goddess
✸ man
✛ woman

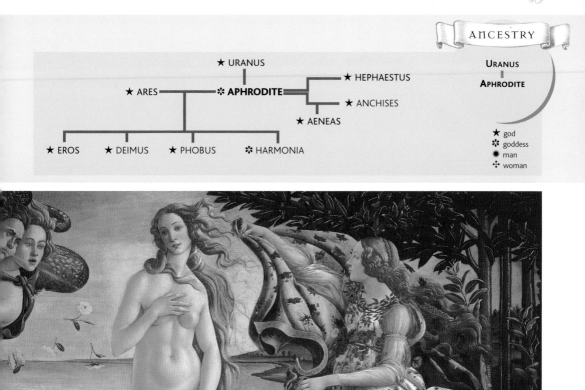

ADONIS, APHRODITE'S REAL LOVE

Aphrodite's overwhelming passion was for Adonis, a god of Asiatic origin. The story of their love affair began when she saved Adonis, a beautiful baby born of an incestuous relationship, by hiding him in a casket which she gave to Persephone for safekeeping. When Aphrodite went to reclaim him, she found that Persephone had opened the casket, admired the child, and decided to keep him for herself. Aphrodite appealed to the gods, and Zeus ruled that Adonis should spend half the year on earth with Aphrodite and half in the Underworld with Persephone.

Adonis was therefore regarded as a god of death and rebirth. During Adonis' annual sojourn in the Underworld, Aphrodite mourned, leaving the earth infertile. Each spring, the goddess of love rediscovered the handsome youth, who was said to return on the first blooming of the red anemone.

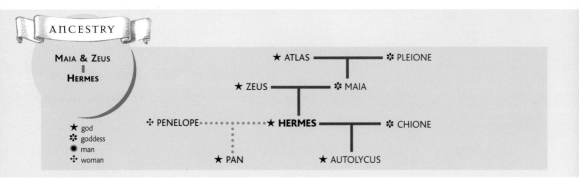

MAIA & ZEUS
|
HERMES

★ ATLAS ——┬—— ❋ PLEIONE

★ ZEUS ——┬—— ❋ MAIA

★ god
❋ goddess
✹ man
✢ woman

✢ PENELOPE ·········· ★ HERMES ——┬—— ❋ CHIONE

★ PAN   ★ AUTOLYCUS

HERMES / MERCURY

Messenger of the gods and escort of the dead to Hades. In Roman mythology, Mercury is the god of trade and commerce.

Hermes was the Arcadian son of Zeus and Maia, the eldest of the Pleiades nymphs born to Atlas and Pleione. Zeus would visit the nymph on Mount Cyllene while his wife Hera was asleep. As the god of travelers, and of good luck in general, Hermes was frequently invoked by the ancient Greeks. He appeared to the adventurer Odysseus on Circe's island in order to warn him of her spells and to advise him how best to overcome them.

Hermes could walk by noon on the day he was born. Soon afterwards, he killed a tortoise and invented the lyre by stretching strings across its shell. This was a fortunate invention, because when he annoyed Apollo by stealing some of his cattle, he was able to offer him the lyre, which had already enchanted the god, and so escape punishment.

THE ARTFUL DODGER

The nimble fingers of Hermes made him the patron of thieves. He stole Apollo's quiver and bow during the hearing of the case regarding the lost cattle. Zeus made Hermes return the items, and Apollo forgave him.

Zeus' wife Hera resented the birth of Hermes. To divert her anger, Hermes dressed himself in swaddling clothes and deceived her into believing that he was her own son, Ares. Having suckled him, Hera then accepted Hermes.

The ploys that Hermes used to aid his fellow gods were ingenious, and Zeus often relied on the winged god's wit. Indeed, Zeus was saved by Hermes in his struggle against Typhon. The creature had cut out Zeus' sinews and hid them in a cave. It took the skill and daring of Hermes to recover them, insert them back into Zeus' limbs, and restore the god to full strength.

MERCURY

Mercury had a stronger association with trade than Hermes. The Latin name derives from Merx, "merchandise." He was renowned for his great speed and the element mercury was named after him.

MERCURY AND ARGUS
Hermes steals Io, in the form of a cow, on Argus' watch.

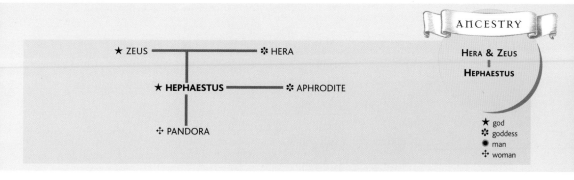

★ ZEUS ——————— ❋ HERA

★ **HEPHAESTUS** ——————— ❋ APHRODITE

✣ PANDORA

HERA & ZEUS

HEPHAESTUS

★ god
❋ goddess
✳ man
✣ woman

HEPHAESTUS/VULCAN

God of fire and of smiths.

Hephaestus was a divine craftsman who built palaces for the gods so they could lead a life of luxury, but his sooty face and limp made him a figure of fun. The story of his life was a series of misfortunes. Twice Hephaestus was flung out of Olympus, the mountain home of the gods. The first time was at birth, when his mother Hera was so disgusted by his dwarfish shape that she cast her baby into the sea, where he would have drowned had he not been saved by the nymphs Thetis and Eurynome.

For nine years the nymphs raised him secretly in a cave and taught him the arts of metalwork. The outcast child then took revenge on his mother. He fashioned a magic throne, or, in another version of the myth, shoes, as a pretend gift for her. Trapped by their power, the great goddess was helpless until Hephaestus agreed to release her. Their reconciliation grew strong and Hera helped her son by setting him up in a fine workshop and arranging a marriage with Aphrodite.

The temperamental Hephaestus, however, became over-confident and was bold enough to criticize his father Zeus for hanging Hera by the wrists from Mount Olympus as a punishment. This brought about Hephaestus' second ejection from the gods' home, when the king of the gods angrily threw the smith down from Olympus. He landed on the island of Lemnos, breaking both legs in the process.

Fortunately, there was a volcano on the island and, despite being lame, Hephaestus set up a forge and taught metalwork to the inhabitants. In time, he was pardoned and reinstated in the god's abode, although by now he could walk only with the aid of golden crutches. One notable achievement of Hephaestus was the creation of Pandora, carried out on Zeus' instructions to take revenge on Prometheus for helping mankind.

THE FIERY VULCAN

The Roman god of fire may take his name from the Latin "volcano" (*Volcanus*), since the Romans believed that Vulcan dwelled in a forge beneath Mount Etna. Sparks flying from the volcano were regarded as eruptions from Vulcan's fiery heart, for he was notorious for his bad temper. From this base the smith produced thunderbolts for Jupiter, king of the gods.

VENUS AND VULCAN
Venus and Vulcan shown with her son Eros and five putti.

DESCENDANTS

OF THE

TITANS

T he Titans were the race of giants who
ruled the universe before Cronus, their
leader, was overthrown by Zeus. There were
twelve Titans and Titanesses, all offspring of
Uranus (Sky) and Gaia (Earth).
The war between Zeus and Cronus
lasted for ten years, after which the
descendants of the Titans mingled with
mortals. The entries in this chapter are
organized by Titan family, excluding the
twelve gods of Olympus. The patriarchs of
the families are Oceanus, Hyperion,
Coeus, Cronus, Crius, and Iapetus.

★ PONTUS

✽ EURYBIA ★ CETO ✽ PHORC'

THE GRAEAE **GORGONS**

✽ DEINO ✽ STHENO ✽ EURYALE

✽ ENYO ✧ **MEDUSA**

✽ PEMPHREDO

Hades abducting Persephone.
See pages 67 and 72

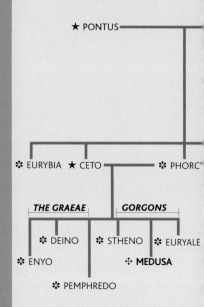

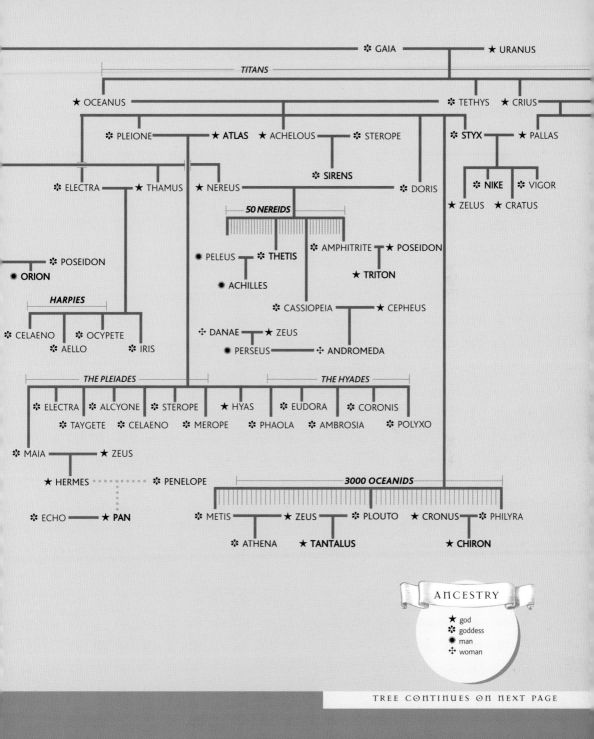

✤ GAIA   ★ URANUS

TITANS

★ OCEANUS   ✤ TETHYS   ★ CRIUS

✤ PLEIONE   ★ **ATLAS**   ★ ACHELOUS   ✤ STEROPE   ✤ **STYX**   ★ PALLAS

✤ **SIRENS**

✤ ELECTRA   ★ THAMUS   ★ NEREUS   ✤ DORIS   ✤ **NIKE**   ✤ VIGOR

★ ZELUS   ★ CRATUS

50 NEREIDS

✤ POSEIDON

✷ **ORION**   ✤ PELEUS   ✤ **THETIS**   ✤ AMPHITRITE   ★ POSEIDON

HARPIES   ✷ **ACHILLES**   ★ **TRITON**

✤ CELAENO   ✤ OCYPETE   ✤ CASSIOPEIA   ★ CEPHEUS

✤ AELLO   ✤ IRIS   ✢ DANAE   ★ ZEUS

✷ PERSEUS   ✢ ANDROMEDA

THE PLEIADES   *THE HYADES*

✤ ELECTRA   ✤ ALCYONE   ✤ STEROPE   ★ HYAS   ✤ EUDORA   ✤ CORONIS

✤ TAYGETE   ✤ CELAENO   ✤ MEROPE   ✤ PHAOLA   ✤ AMBROSIA   ✤ POLYXO

✤ MAIA   ★ ZEUS

★ HERMES   ✤ PENELOPE   *3000 OCEANIDS*

✤ ECHO   ★ **PAN**   ✤ METIS   ★ ZEUS   ✤ PLOUTO   ★ CRONUS   ✤ PHILYRA

✤ ATHENA   ★ **TANTALUS**   ★ **CHIRON**

ANCESTRY

★ god
✤ goddess
✷ man
✢ woman

TREE CONTINUES ON NEXT PAGE

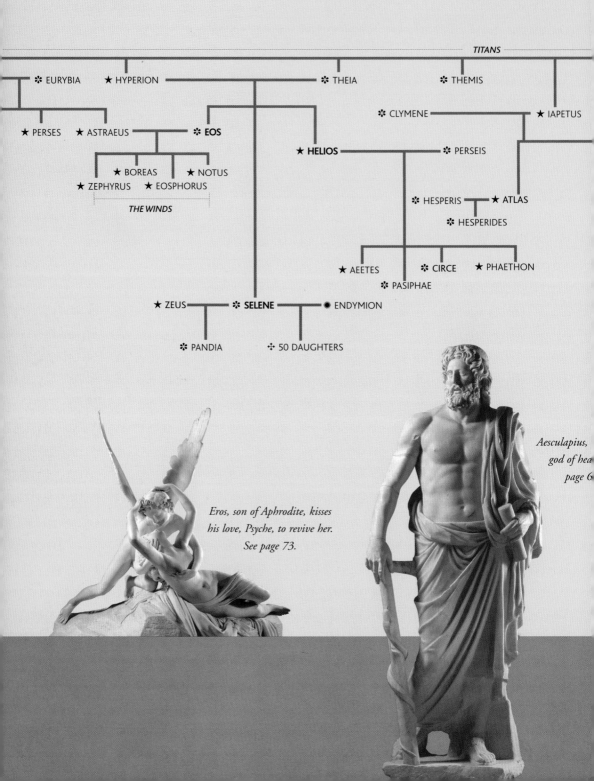

TITANS

❋ EURYBIA ★ HYPERION ━━━ ❋ THEIA ❋ THEMIS

❋ CLYMENE ★ IAPETUS

★ PERSES ★ ASTRAEUS ━━━ ❋ **EOS** ★ **HELIOS** ━━━ ❋ PERSEIS

★ BOREAS ★ NOTUS
★ ZEPHYRUS ❋ EOSPHORUS ❋ HESPERIS ━━ ★ ATLAS

THE WINDS ❋ HESPERIDES

★ AEETES ❋ CIRCE ★ PHAETHON

❋ PASIPHAE

★ ZEUS ━━━ ❋ **SELENE** ━━━ ✺ ENDYMION

❋ PANDIA ✢ 50 DAUGHTERS

*Eros, son of Aphrodite, kisses
his love, Psyche, to revive her.
See page 73.*

*Aesculapius,
god of hea
page 6*

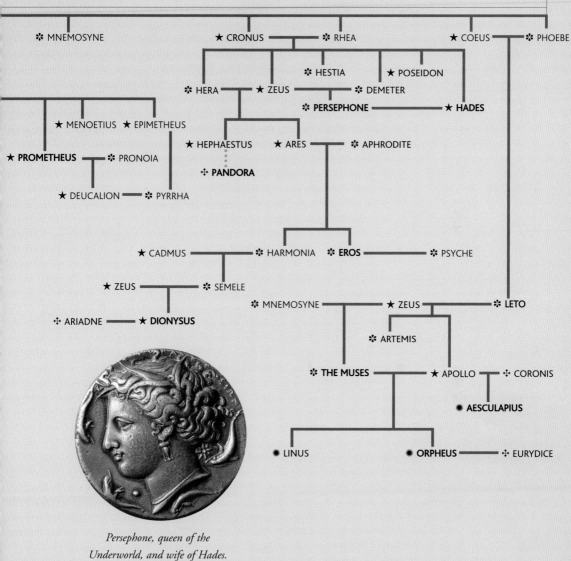

❈ MNEMOSYNE   ★ CRONUS ——— ❈ RHEA   ★ COEUS ——— ❈ PHOEBE

                              ❈ HESTIA   ★ POSEIDON

              ❈ HERA ——— ★ ZEUS   ❈ DEMETER

                                   ❈ PERSEPHONE ——————— ★ HADES

★ MENOETIUS ❈ EPIMETHEUS

                              ★ HEPHAESTUS   ★ ARES ——— ❈ APHRODITE

★ PROMETHEUS ——— ❈ PRONOIA

                              ✤ PANDORA

       ★ DEUCALION ——— ❈ PYRRHA

                              ★ CADMUS ——————— ❈ HARMONIA   ❈ EROS ——————— ❈ PSYCHE

              ★ ZEUS ——— ❈ SEMELE

✤ ARIADNE ——— ★ DIONYSUS

                    ❈ MNEMOSYNE ——————— ★ ZEUS ——————— ❈ LETO

                                        ❈ ARTEMIS

                    ❈ THE MUSES ——————— ★ APOLLO ——— ✤ CORONIS

                                              ☀ AESCULAPIUS

                    ☀ LINUS   ☀ ORPHEUS ——— ✤ EURYDICE

*Persephone, queen of the
Underworld, and wife of Hades.*
See page 72.

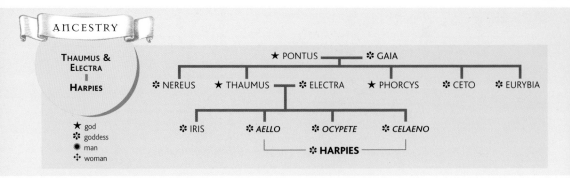

THAUMUS &
ELECTRA
|
HARPIES

★ PONTUS — ✻ GAIA

✻ NEREUS ★ THAUMUS — ✻ ELECTRA ★ PHORCYS ✻ CETO ✻ EURYBIA

★ god
✻ goddess
☀ man
✣ woman

✻ IRIS ✻ *AELLO* ✻ *OCYPETE* ✻ *CELAENO*

✻ **HARPIES**

HARPIES

*Predatory monsters with a vulture's body, wings, and claws,
and a woman's head.*

The daughters of the sea god Thaumas, known as the Harpies, had insatiable hungers. Their name means "snatchers" because they would swoop down and take food from dining tables, at the same time fouling any scraps that remained with the stench of their breath. Hence, they were regarded as harbingers of starvation and death.

JASON'S ENCOUNTER WITH THE HARPIES

In the legendary stories of Jason, the Argonauts—a group of heroes engaged with Jason in the quest for the Golden Fleece— once docked at a port in Thrace, ruled by King Phineus. He was constantly pestered by the wretched Harpies, who would swoop down at every meal and take his food, leaving him half-starved. Although the king was blind, he had the gift of foresight, and when Jason asked him how he could find the Golden Fleece, he replied that first the Harpies had to be destroyed.

When a banquet was prepared for Jason, the Harpies appeared as usual to steal the food. However, Calais and Zetes, the winged sons of Boreas, god of the North Wind, pursued the dreadful creatures through the air and drove them out to sea. Some versions of the story say that Calais and Zetes caught up with the monsters and were about to kill them when the messenger god Iris intervened on their behalf, promising that if the Harpies were spared, they would return to their cave on Crete and stay there forever. Happily liberated from the curse of the Harpies, King Phineus told Jason how his quest for the Golden Fleece was destined to turn out.

IN ART

In ancient art, the Harpies always appear with women's faces. They also appear in Dante's *Inferno*, where they are depicted mutilating those who have committed suicide and been turned into trees.

HARPIES ATTACKING MEN AND WOMEN
From an early 14th-century manuscript Voyage of Saint Louis into Purgatory, *from San Patrizio. Here, the Harpies are portrayed in a more dragon-like form than they would have been depicted in ancient times.*

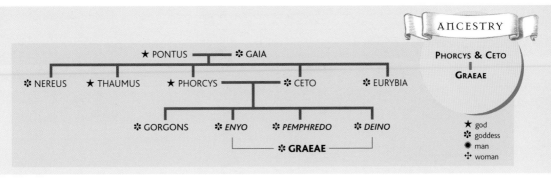

★ PONTUS ——— ❊ GAIA

❊ NEREUS   ★ THAUMUS   ★ PHORCYS ——— ❊ CETO   ❊ EURYBIA

❊ GORGONS   ❊ ENYO   ❊ PEMPHREDO   ❊ DEINO

❊ GRAEAE

★ god
❊ goddess
✳ man
✢ woman

GRAEAE

The three weird sisters of the Gorgons: Enyo (warlike),
Pemphredo (waspish), and Deino (terrible).

From birth, these swan-like women, whose Greek name means the "gray ones" on account of their gray hair, possessed only one eye and one tooth, which they shared and passed between them by hand. Most of the legends in which they appear involve Perseus, son of Zeus, who was given the seemingly impossible task of fetching the head of the Gorgon Medusa.

In order to succeed in his quest, Perseus had to find a pair of winged sandals, a cap of invisibility, and a magic wallet in which to carry Medusa's head. However, all these items were possessed by the Stygian nymphs, and only the Graeae knew their whereabouts.

Perseus therefore went in search of these three dangerous creatures who lived at the foot of Mount Atlas, where they resided on thrones. Their swan-like appearance derived from their association with destruction (the swan being the mythological bird of death). Perseus lay in wait for the sisters and, when they were passing their single eye and single tooth between them, he snatched their vital possessions. Using them as a bribe, Perseus demanded to know where the Stygian nymphs lived. Having acquired the information he needed, Perseus threw the eye into Lake Tritonis so that the Graeae would be unable to warn the nymphs of his approach. Eventually, having collected the items he required from the nymphs, Perseus continued his journey and was successful in cutting off Medusa's head.

PERSEUS AND
THE GRAIAE
This painting
by Sir Edward
Burne-Jones,
1876, shows
Perseus stealing
the only eye and
tooth that the
Graeae possess.

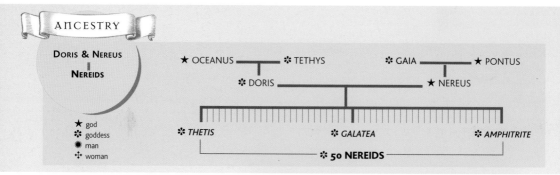

ANCESTRY

DORIS & NEREUS
|
NEREIDS

★ god
❈ goddess
✳ man
✣ woman

★ OCEANUS ——— ❈ TETHYS   ❈ GAIA ——— ★ PONTUS

❈ DORIS ——————————————————— ★ NEREUS

❈ THETIS   ❈ GALATEA   ❈ AMPHITRITE

❈ 50 NEREIDS

NEREIDS

Nymphs of the sea.

Nymphs of all kinds— whether of the sea, rivers, or woods— were young, beautiful, amorous, and gentle. But, like gods and mortals, nymphs also had their dark side, a wild characteristic by which they could be vengeful and destructive.

The Nereids were fifty daughters of Nereus, who lived in the depths of the Mediterranean Sea, usually tending to the needs of the immortal sea-nymph Thetis. They were believed to be priestesses of the moon and had the power to ensure successful fishing.

In one legend concerning the Nereids, Cassiopeia, who was married to Cepheus, King of Joppa, claimed that their daughter Andromeda was more beautiful than the Nereids. They complained to their protector Poseidon, who then sent a flood to Philistia (where Joppa was located) and unleashed a monster on its people. When King Cepheus consulted the Oracle of Ammon to find out how he could escape the terrible

vengeance imposed on his subjects, he was told to sacrifice his daughter to the sea monster.

He therefore chained Andromeda, naked but for a few jewels, to a cliff on the coast, and waited anxiously with his wife to see the monster devour their daughter. At that time Perseus was flying overhead as he escaped from the Gorgons and noticed the forlorn figure chained to the rock in all her radiant beauty. Perseus was immediately struck by Andromeda's beauty and

NEREID ON A MERHORSE
A Thracian harness ornament.

swooped down in his winged sandals and rescued her.

Ones of the Nereids, Amphitrite, was said to have become Queen of the Sea when she married Poseidon, causing some jealousy among the mermaids. The Nereids were also known to have helped Jason and the Argonauts to steer their ship away from Scylla and Charybdis, and the Clashing Rocks.

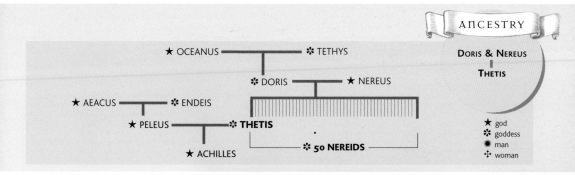

DORIS & NEREUS

THETIS

★ OCEANUS ——— ❈ TETHYS

❈ DORIS ——— ★ NEREUS

★ AEACUS ——— ❈ ENDEIS

★ PELEUS ——— ❈ THETIS

★ ACHILLES ❈ **50 NEREIDS**

★ god
❈ goddess
✳ man
✣ woman

THETIS

Most important of the Nereid sea-nymphs and immortal mother of Achilles.

The Fates prophesied that Thetis would bear a son who would become more powerful than his father. Zeus desired Thetis until he learned about this prophesy, but was annoyed nevertheless by her rejection of his advances. Zeus vowed that Thetis should not marry an immortal, and instead chose a mortal king, Peleus of Iolcus. The wedding feast was disrupted by Eris, the goddess of strife, who was angry that she was not an invited guest. In an act of petulance, she threw down an apple on which was inscribed "To the fairest." Hera, Athena, and Aphrodite each wished to claim the prize, and their ensuing dispute ultimately led to the Trojan War.

Thetis and Peleus had seven sons. To discover whether they had inherited their mother's immortality, Thetis anointed her first six sons in ambrosia before burning their mortal parts. None survived. Wishing to spare their seventh son the same fate, Peleus asked the centaur Chiron to take

care of Achilles. Thetis dipped Achilles in the River Styx to make him invulnerable, but the water did not touch the spot where she held him by the heel. Blessed with the gift of prophecy, Thetis often visited Achilles and comforted him during the Trojan War, but she could not prevent his death at Troy when a poisoned arrow struck the one vulnerable part of his body— his heel.

LIFEGUARD AT SEA

When mortals fell afoul of fortune at sea and were in danger of drowning, Thetis would often come to their rescue. When the infant Hephaestus was hurled from

MAKNG ACHILLES IMMORTAL
Thetis immerses her son Achilles in the water of the River Styx in order to make him invulnerable.

Mount Olympus by his mother Hera when she saw how ugly he was, it was Thetis who took him to her cave on the island of Lemnos and nursed him back to health. At Thetis' request, Hephaestus made a set of armor for her son Achilles to protect him during the Trojan War. And it was Thetis who saved Jason and the Argonauts from the monster Scylla and whirlpool Charybdis by tossing their ship from side to side, thereby avoiding their reach.

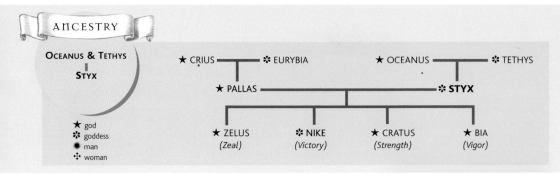

ANCESTRY

OCEANUS & TETHYS
|
STYX

★ god
❋ goddess
☀ man
♻ woman

★ CRIUS ——— ❋ EURYBIA   ★ OCEANUS ——— ❋ TETHYS

★ PALLAS ———————————————— ❋ STYX

★ ZELUS   ❋ NIKE   ★ CRATUS   ★ BIA
(Zeal)   (Victory)   (Strength)   (Vigor)

STYX

*A river that encircled the Underworld of Hades,
across which the souls of the dead were ferried
from the land of the living.*

As river-goddess of the Underworld and a daughter of Oceanus, Styx was honored by the Olympians for helping Zeus to defeat the Titans, even though she was married to the Titan Pallas. Oaths sworn in her name bound deities to their word.

Ghosts hovered over the cool, sluggish waters of the Styx. Corpses floated by as Charon ferried the newly dead across the river from the land of the living to their final resting place in the Underworld. Corpses raised their putrid hands and pleaded to be hauled into the boat, but the passengers were forbidden to help those who had not paid.

PSYCHE'S VISIT

When Venus sent Pysche to the Underworld on an uncertain mission, three women were waiting on the banks of the Styx to greet her as she disembarked from the ferryboat. Placed there to trick Psyche, the women were weaving cloth and asking for help. Only by resisting their requests was Psyche able to leave the Underworld.

Others who succeeded in crossing the Styx and returning to the land of the living included Orpheus and Aeneas, who was directed by the Cumaean Sibyl to reach the Golden Bough so that he might return from the Underworld.

CHARON THE FERRYMAN

Charon, a scruffy old man who demanded a fee for every ride in his patched-up boat, ferried the newly dead across the Styx to the Underworld. Charon expected payment from every passenger because the god Avarice lived nearby. A poor man who could not afford the fee to cross the river was not allowed true death, but was forced to wander in misery on the banks of the river forever. In ancient Greece, corpses were usually buried with a coin lodged underneath each eye to pay Charon for their safe passage across the Styx. Sometimes the ferryman was depicted as a winged demon holding a double hammer. The medieval writer Dante portrayed Charon in his epic poem the *Divine Comedy* as the first character the dead encounter when they enter hell.

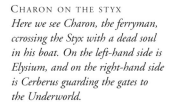

CHARON ON THE STYX
*Here we see Charon, the ferryman,
ccrossing the Styx with a dead soul
in his boat. On the left-hand side is
Elysium, and on the right-hand side
is Cerberus guarding the gates to
the Underworld.*

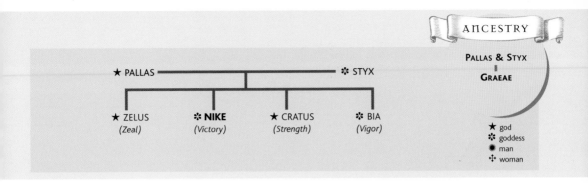

★ PALLAS ———————— ✢ STYX

★ ZELUS
(Zeal)

✢ **NIKE**
(Victory)

★ CRATUS
(Strength)

✢ BIA
(Vigor)

PALLAS & STYX
|
GRAEAE

★ god
✢ goddess
✵ man
✢ woman

N I K E

Winged goddess of victory who fought with the Olympian gods against the Titans; known as Victoria by the Romans.

The marriage between the River Styx and Pallas the Titan produced a number of powerful offspring: Nike (Victory), Zelus (Zeal), Cratus (Strength), and Bia (Vigor). Nike inspired athletes and musicians when they participated in competitions. She often assisted Zeus and Athena, and presided over contests, crowning the winner with a wreath or palm. Unusually for a goddess, Nike possessed no special powers of her own. Her main attribute was speed, and she brought good luck and often helped other gods in their missions. Her closeness to Athena was demonstrated by the small temple dedicated to the two goddesses on the Acropolis in Athens. Part of the frieze brought by the Earl of Elgin to England in the early 1800s included a relief of Nike celebrating the victory of the Greeks over the Persians. This is now displayed in the British Museum in London.

The Roman goddess, known as Victoria, took on a more serious and warlike role. She was associated with the cults of Jupiter and Mars, and was worshiped by Roman soldiers.

IN ART
The "Winged Victory of Samothrace," one of the finest surviving Greek sculptures which is displayed in the Louvre in Paris, shows the goddess missing her head and arms. Other artistic representations of Nike, such as those painted on Greek vases, depict her bearing a wreath, jug, phial, or censer, indicating her involvement with temple rituals. In some parts of Italy Victoria was portrayed as a charioteer, and elsewhere she was shown brandishing weapons and trophies of victory in battle.

WINGED VICTORY OF SAMOTHRACE
Before losing her arms, Nike was probably blowing a victory paean on a trumpet.

THE GORGONS

Monstrous sisters with wings, claws, and serpent hair, the most famous being Medusa.

Of these monstrous sisters, Euryale (Wide-roaming) and Stheno (Strong) were immortal, but Medusa (Ruler) was mortal. All three were so hideous that a mere glance at one of them could turn a person into stone.

It is in the story of Perseus that Medusa reared her ugly head. This son of Danae and Zeus had been adopted by King Polydectes after the boy and his mother were washed onto his island. Now, the king had designs to marry Danae against her will. Perseus offered to win whatever gift the bridegroom desired, even the head of Medusa if he so wished, as long as Polydectes married Hippodameia, his official bride, and not Danae. Polydectes accepted this rash gesture, and asked Perseus to bring back Medusa's head—a seemingly impossible task.

The goddess Athena overheard the conversation and, as an enemy of the Gorgons, she offered to help Perseus in his mission. She took him to the island of Samos where all three Gorgons could be seen in pictorial form, so that he could tell Medusa apart from her immortal sisters. Athena warned Perseus not to set eyes directly on Medusa or he would be turned to stone. To aid him in his mission, she gave him a highly polished shield.

The winged god Hermes, patron of travelers, lent Perseus a sickle with which to cut off the Gorgon's head. Well-prepared for the task, he set off for the western land of the Hyperboreans where the Gorgons dwelt. Perseus approached stealthily as the monstrous sisters slept among their victims—men and beasts who had been petrified. Looking only at the image of Medusa reflected in his shield, Perseus raised his sickle and with one blow sliced off her head. As her sisters stirred, Perseus quickly hid the head with its serpent hair in a wallet and took flight with the aid of winged sandals lent to him by nymphs. The speed and nimbleness of the sandals enabled Perseus to outstrip the enraged pursuing Gorgons. As Perseus flew over the desert, some drops of Medusa's blood fell onto the sand, and swarms of poisonous snakes emerged.

MEDUSA SLAIN
The head of Medusa, with snakes for hair.

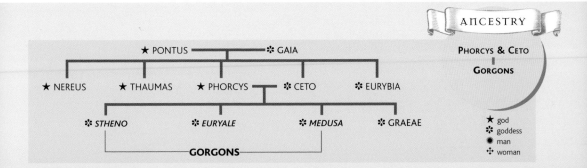

ANCESTRY

PHORCYS & CETO

GORGONS

★ PONTUS ━━━━━ ❈ GAIA

★ NEREUS   ★ THAUMAS   ★ PHORCYS ━ ❈ CETO   ❈ EURYBIA

❈ *STHENO*   ❈ *EURYALE*   ❈ *MEDUSA*   ❈ *GRAEAE*

GORGONS

★ god
❈ goddess
✳ man
✢ woman

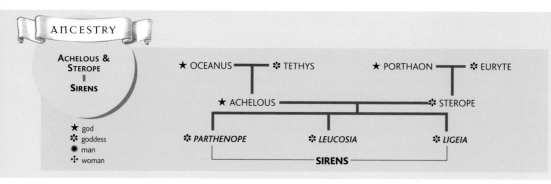

ACHELOUS & STEROPE

SIRENS

★ god
❖ goddess
✳ man
⚶ woman

★ OCEANUS — ❖ TETHYS   ★ PORTHAON — ❖ EURYTE

★ ACHELOUS ━━━━━━━ ❖ STEROPE

❖ *PARTHENOPE*   ❖ *LEUCOSIA*   ❖ *LIGEIA*

SIRENS

SIRENS

Sea-nymphs in the form of huge birds with women's heads.

The Sirens, who in various accounts numbered between two and five, were similar creatures to the Harpies. They lived on an island off the coast of Sicily surrounded by dangerous rocks. Their sweet song was so enchanting that seafarers were lured by its sound toward the island, becoming shipwrecked on the rocks. Although Odysseus had been warned of the danger by Circe, he was nevertheless curious to hear the Sirens' beautiful song. To ensure that his crew would not be mesmerized by the sound, he ordered them to block their ears with wax and to bind him to the ship's mast. When, however, Odysseus heard the Sirens' captivating singing, he begged the sailors to untie him, but they refused. Odysseus was only released when the ship had sailed so far away from the Sirens' island that their song could no longer be heard. He was the only man who heard the Sirens' song and survived.

In another episode, Jason and the Argonauts were saved from destruction by the music of Orpheus, whom Chiron had advised Jason to take on the journey for protection. When his ship, the *Argo*, approached the dreaded rocks and Orpheus heard the first strains of the fateful singing, he outplayed the Sirens on his lyre, thus preventing their song from reaching the ears of the crew.

In some versions of the story, the Sirens were believed to be the playmates of Persephone, queen of the Underworld. Elsewhere, it was said that Aphrodite, goddess of love, had transformed some recalcitrant women into birds for not yielding their virginity to either the gods or men. The unfortunate creatures had no power of flight, however, because the Muses had defeated them in a singing contest and plucked their wing feathers to make themselves crowns. Thus, the Sirens could only perch and sing among the bones of their victims.

Today, the term "siren song" refers to an appeal that is hard to resist but, if heeded, will inevitably lead to a person's downfall.

ODYSSEUS AND THE SIRENS
A 3rd-century Roman mosaic from Tunisia showing Odysseus tied to the ship's mast to survive the Sirens' song.

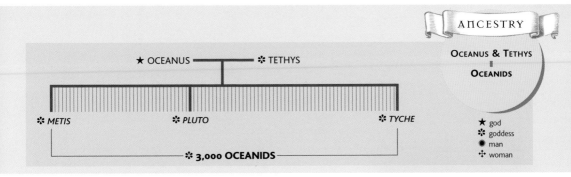

ANCESTRY

OCEANUS & TETHYS

OCEANIDS

★ OCEANUS ──────── ✳ TETHYS

✳ METIS   ✳ PLUTO   ✳ TYCHE

✳ **3,000 OCEANIDS**

★ god
✳ goddess
✳ man
✢ woman

OCEANIDS

Three thousand sea-nymphs in Greek and Roman mythology.

Nymphs were neither deities nor immortal, but female spirits of nature with a very long lifespan. Each one of these three thousand daughters of the Titans Oceanus and Tethys became a patron of a particular body of water, whether a spring, river, pond, lake, or sea. As young women with a zest for life, they frequently fell in love with mortals, but they were also pursued by Zeus and other gods.

One Oceanid, Metis, adopted various guises to avoid Zeus' advances, but eventually she succumbed and became his wife. Gaia warned Metis that after giving birth to the baby girl in her womb, she would bear a son who would usurp her husband's position in heaven. Anxious to prevent this, Zeus swallowed his pregnant wife. Nevertheless, she continued to thrive inside him and when the time was ripe for the birth of her child, the smith god Hephaestus split open Zeus' head with an axe, and Athena emerged, fully armed.

Tyche was a powerful nymph who possessed a talent for determining fortune. Having a playful cast of mind, she delighted in producing unpredictable outcomes, and would offer help to her unsuspecting victims by demonstrating examples of her amazing ability to effect changes in people's fortunes.

OCEANUS, FATHER OF THE NYMPH

This Titan son of Gaia and Uranus fathered all the water gods and nymphs, except Poseidon. Oceanus was a kindly old man with a long beard and the horns of a bull. He also personified the river of the same name that was believed to encircle the earth. All rivers were believed to flow from it, just as the sun rose from it and the moon sank into it.

Tethys, wife of Oceanus, gave birth to the rivers of the Underworld, including the Styx.

SEA CENTAURS AND OCEANIDS
Relief on a 3rd-century Roman sarcophagus showing various sea-nymphs and nereids.

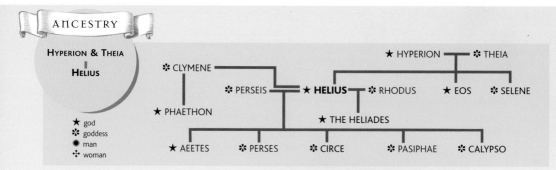
H E L I U S

God of the sun.

Helius left his palace in the east in the morning and crossed the sky in a golden chariot drawn by four horses; he rested in his western palace in the evening and then sailed back to the east via the River Oceanus at night. His chief cult was at Rhodes, the island Zeus gave him to compensate for the fact that he was forgotten when the universe was divided up.

In one myth, Helius played an important part in the war between the giants and the gods. By obeying Zeus' order to stay out of the sky, Helius prevented the earth goddess Gaia from growing an herb that would have made the giants immortal. As a result, they were vulnerable to heroes such as Heracles.

PHAETHON AND THE SOLAR CHARIOT

The myth of Helius' son Phaethon is as important as any concerning the sun god himself. Phaethon wished to be convinced that he was actually Helius' son, so he traveled to his father's dazzling palace to ask him.

Putting his powerful solar rays aside to avoid scorching his son, Helius greeted him warmly and promised him a gift of his choice. Phaethon's greatest desire was to ride the sun chariot for a day. Bound by his word, Helius reluctantly agreed, although he knew that the undertaking was fraught with danger.

Mounting the chariot, Phaethon proudly took hold of the horses' reins and set off across the sky. The horses soon sensed the charioteer's inexperience, however, and bolted down toward the earth. The terrified

HELIUS IN
HIS CHARIOT
*A Greek bowl
depicting Helius riding
his chariot, drawn by horses
and accompanied by dolphins.*

youth lost control and the horses took the chariot so close to the earth that it scorched a fertile plain, turning it to desert. The inhabitants were also burnt and their skins remained black forever. Zeus, anxious for the earth's safety, intervened. Phaethon was flung from the chariot by a thunderbolt and hurtled down to earth in a ball of flames. His corpse fell into the River Eridanus and the chariot was drenched with rain.

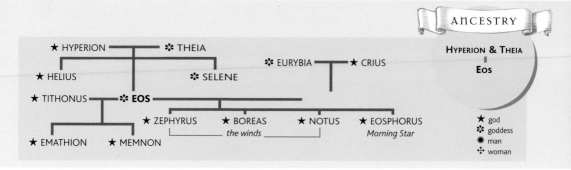

★ HYPERION — ❋ THEIA

❋ EURYBIA — ★ CRIUS

★ HELIUS   ❋ SELENE

★ TITHONUS — ❋ EOS

★ ZEPHYRUS   ★ BOREAS   ★ NOTUS   ★ EOSPHORUS

the winds   *Morning Star*

★ EMATHION   ★ MEMNON

★ god
❋ goddess
✳ man
✢ woman

EOS / AURORA

Greek goddess of the dawn, known to the Romans as Aurora.

Eos was the daughter of the Titans Hyperion and Theia. Each morning, she would drive across the sky in a chariot pulled by two fine horses, Phaethon (Shiner) and Lampos (Bright). She would ride to Mount Olympus, home of the gods, and announce the rising of her brother Helius (Sun) and the fading of her sister Selene (Moon). Eos herself was usually depicted with wings, and by coupling with Astraeus (Dawn Wind) became mother to the three other winds—Zephyrus (West), Boreas (North), and Notus (South)—and to the stars, including Eosphorus (Morning Star).

NYMPHOMANIA

Eos was an amorous goddess who kidnaped most of her young lovers. Her legend is mostly concerned with the intrigues of these escapades. First she slept

with Ares, an affair that so annoyed Aphrodite that she turned Eos into a nymphomaniac as a punishment. Shamefaced, she seduced lover after lover, including the giant Orion (son of Poseidon), whom she took to Delos, and Cephalus, whom she carried off to Syria.

A final abduction involved a young Trojan, Tithonus, who became her favorite and with whom she had two sons, one of whom was the Trojan War hero Memnon. She pleaded with Zeus to grant Tithonus immortality, but unfortunately forgot to ask that he be made

eternally young as well. To her dismay, she found that she had to keep him into his old age. Some said that Tithonus, who was kept miserably imprisoned in Eos' palace, grew so disfigured with age that he lost the appearance of a man and turned into a desiccated cicada.

IN ART

Eos is portrayed in both art and literature driving her horse-drawn chariot across the sky. One of the carvings on the pediments of the Parthenon in Athens, now displayed in the British Museum in London, bears the head of one of her horses. Sometimes she is depicted with rosy fingers opening the gates of heaven to allow the sun's chariot to enter.

TITHONUS AND EOS
An 18th-century painting depicting Eos with Tithonus and some of her many suitors.

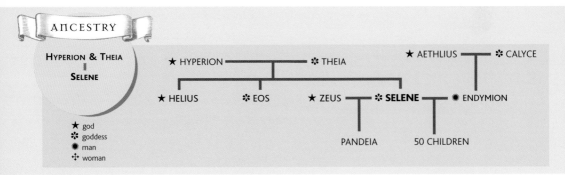

HYPERION & THEIA
|
SELENE

★ HYPERION ——— ✿ THEIA

★ AETHLIUS ——— ✿ CALYCE

★ HELIUS   ✿ EOS   ★ ZEUS ——— ✿ **SELENE** ——— ✹ ENDYMION

★ god
✿ goddess
✹ man
✤ woman

PANDEIA   50 CHILDREN

SELENE/LUNA

Ancient Greek moon goddess, known to the Romans as Luna.

After her brother Helius (Sun) had finished crossing the sky, Selene would rise as night fell upon the earth. Like Helius, she would drive across the sky in a horse-drawn chariot. Together, they determined the temperature of the air and were associated with healing diseases and preventing death. In later mythology, Selene was absorbed into both Artemis, protector of childbirth, and Hecate, goddess of the Underworld. She was also skilled in the art of sorcery and love charms.

Selene bore Zeus a daughter and then fell in love with a handsome shepherd named Endymion, a son of Zeus and the nymph Calyce. She was attracted to him when she saw him asleep in a cave on Mount Latmus in Ionia. She lay down beside him and gently kissed his eyes. They had fifty daughters (including Naxos), but Selene

did not wish her mortal lover to die, so she put him to sleep forever. Another version of the story says that Endymion was granted a wish and he chose eternal sleep in which he would neither age nor die. Eventually, he was taken to heaven by Zeus.

A further legend tells how Selene was seduced by Pan who disguised his hairy goatskin with a white fleece. Duped, Selene rode on his back and let him do as he pleased with her.

The Roman goddess was represented in three regions of the universe: Luna in the heavens, Diana on earth, and Hecate in the Underworld. There were three phases of the lunar cycle: Diana was the crescent-shaped moon, Selene the full moon, and Hecate the darkness when the moon was not visible.

SELENE AND ENDYMION
Selene could not bear for the mortal Endymion to die, so she put him to sleep, and watched over him forever.

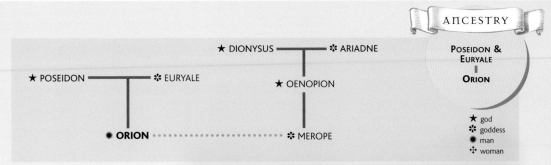

ANCESTRY

★ DIONYSUS ━━━━ ❖ ARIADNE

★ POSEIDON ━━━━ ❖ EURYALE

★ OENOPION

**POSEIDON &
EURYALE**

ORION

✹ ORION ∙∙∙∙∙∙∙∙∙∙∙∙∙∙∙∙∙∙∙∙∙∙∙∙ ❖ MEROPE

★ god
❖ goddess
✹ man
✛ woman

ORION

*Giant hunter renowned for
his good looks; said by some
to have been born from the
earth, with a gigantic body,
and by others to be the son
of Poseidon and Euryale.*

ORION PURSUES PLEIADES
*An 18th-century engraving
showing Pleiades pursued by
the giant Orion.*

At one time, the island of
Chios in the Aegean Sea
was overrun by wild
animals. Its king, Oenopion,
promised Orion that if he could
rid the island of all the beasts he
would allow him to marry his
daughter Merope. When Orion
had completed the task, he went
to the king to claim his trophy
bride. However, Oenopion went
back on his word, maintaining
that there were still bears and
wolves at large, and refused to
part with his daughter.

In frustration, Orion forced
his way into Merope's bedroom
when he was drunk and raped
her. When Oenopion discovered
what had happened, he enlisted
the help of his father Dionysus,
who ordered satyrs to ply Orion
with more wine so that he would
sink into a deep sleep. Then
Oenopion exacted his revenge
and put out both of Orion's eyes
while the hunter slept.

Distraught, Orion sought
advice from an oracle who told
him that his sight would be
restored if he went east to where
Helius rose. So he rowed to the
island of Lemnos, where he
entered the forge of Hephaestus
and hired a guide who led him
over land and sea to the furthest
point of the ocean. In a great
turn of fortune, Orion not only
had his sight restored by Helius,
but he also found that Eos,
goddess of the dawn, had fallen
in love with him.

ARTEMIS AND LOVE OF
THE CHASE

While he was trying to find
Oenopion to seek his revenge,
Orion met Artemis who shared
his love of hunting. Together
they thrilled in the chase of wild
animals. Having seen how Eos
had lost her heart to Orion,

Artemis' brother Apollo was
worried that the same might
happen to his sister. He devised a
plan and set a giant scorpion in
pursuit of Orion. The hunter
found that he could not pierce
the creature's armor and he fled
to seek the protection of Eos.
Apollo then tricked Artemis by
challenging her to shoot an
arrow at a black object bobbing
in the sea. At first, Artemis was
delighted with her accuracy, but
later was dismayed to discover
that her arrow had pierced
Orion's skull. In her grief,
Artemis set his image among the
stars in the sky, and it can still be
seen, pursued by the Scorpion.

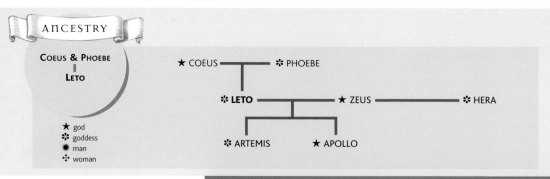

ANCESTRY

COEUS & PHOEBE
|
LETO

★ COEUS ━━━┳━━━ ❀ PHOEBE

★ god
❀ goddess
✳ man
✢ woman

❀ **LETO** ━━━━━━━━┳━━━━━━━ ★ ZEUS ━━━━━━━━ ❀ HERA

❀ ARTEMIS   ★ APOLLO

The birth of Leto's twins, Artemis and Apollo, is the main theme of her mythology. Zeus' future wife Hera became jealous of the god's passion for the beautiful Titaness. To prevent her from coming to any harm, Zeus turned himself and Leto into quails before they coupled, and then she flew away.

Determined not to be humiliated, Hera sent the serpent Python in pursuit of Leto, who was thus prevented from coming to land to give birth. Other versions of the story say that she was forced to wander pregnant for months, as no land would accept her for fear of the wrath of Hera, who had forbidden any place to receive Leto's offspring.

With the help of the South Wind, Leto eventually came to Delos, a floating island in the Cyclades, where she was able to land safely. (Delos allowed Leto to land on its island on condition that it became rooted to the earth, and this request was granted.) On touching down, she was turned back into a woman

by Zeus and finally gave birth to the first of her twins, Artemis. The baby daughter helped her mother find a place to deliver the second child, Apollo, who was born after nine days and nights of dreadful pain. It is said that Artemis was so traumatized by this experience that she told Zeus that she wished never to

LETO AND HER FAMILY
An ancient relief depicting Leto with her children, Apollo and Artemis, and their father, Zeus.

experience giving birth again, but she wanted instead to remain a virgin and to help pregnant women give birth.

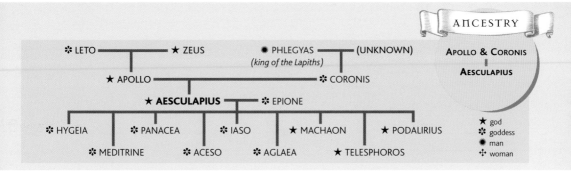

❋ LETO ──── ★ ZEUS   ✹ PHLEGYAS ──── (UNKNOWN)   **APOLLO & CORONIS**
                      (king of the Lapiths)
                                                   AESCULAPIUS

★ APOLLO ──────────────────────── ❋ CORONIS

★ **AESCULAPIUS** ──── ❋ EPIONE

❋ HYGEIA   ❋ PANACEA   ❋ IASO   ★ MACHAON   ★ PODALIRIUS   ★ god
                                                                ❋ goddess
   ❋ MEDITRINE   ❋ ACESO   ❋ AGLAEA   ★ TELESPHOROS   ✹ man
                                                                ✥ woman

AESCULAPIUS

Greek god of healing and principal deity concerned with prophecy and divination.

Aesculapius suffered a violent start to life. His mother Coronis was loved by his father Apollo, but she made him angry by being unfaithful while she was carrying Aesculapius in her womb. Unable to tolerate the infidelity, Apollo asked his sister Artemis to slay Coronis but, wishing to save his son, he tore the unborn child from his mother's womb as she burned on the funeral pyre.

Aesculapius was brought up by Chiron, the gentlest of the Centaurs, beastlike monsters who lived in the woods. Chiron was renowned for his wisdom and wide knowledge, which covered all the arts and sciences, and he taught Aesculapius the secrets of medicine.

In time, Aesculapius married and settled down to family life. But it was said that he drew the wrath of Zeus upon himself by daring to bring the dead back to life. Zeus struck Aesculapius with a thunderbolt and killed him.

Aesculapius' father avenged this act by killing Zeus' sons, the one-eyed giant Cyclopes. As a punishment, Apollo was forced to become a slave for a year and serve a mortal king.

The slaying of Aesculapius, and indeed the question of his death, has remained something of a mystery. He seems to have been a hero who attained divinity. His cult, like that of Apollo, included prophecy, but he was essentially concerned with prescribing courses of medical treatment. He was closely associated with snakes and is usually portrayed as a bearded man in early middle age, holding a serpent.

The Greek poet Homer says that Aesculapius had talented sons who were competent medical healers.

ROMAN STATUE OF AESCULAPIUS
Aesculapius is traditionally depicted as a bearded man wearing a robe that leaves his chest uncovered. He holds a staff with his sacred single serpent coiled around it, symbolizing the renewal of youth as the serpent casts off its skin.

ORPHEUS

Legendary Greek poet and musician.

As son of Apollo and Calliope, the poetic member of the Muses, Orpheus was blessed with musical talent. Whenever he sang and played the lyre, all creation would listen, entranced. It was said that his playing was even able to physically move trees and rocks. During the adventures of Jason and the Argonauts, Orpheus helped the sailors to avoid the Sirens and Clashing Rocks by playing his lyre.

CHARMING HADES

When his wife Eurydice was bitten by a snake and died, Orpheus descended to the Underworld and won the hearts of many there by his playing—the damned forgot the agony of their tortures and even Hades, god of the dead and the Underworld was moved to weep iron tears. In gratitude, Hades granted Orpheus a favor by allowing him to recover Eurydice, but only on one condition: he must lead her out of the Underworld without looking back until they had reached the surface of the earth. As they were about to emerge into the light, Orpheus forgot the condition and glanced back at his wife. Immediately Eurydice turned into a wraith and vanished. Unable to re-enter the

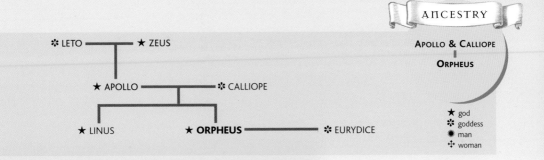

APOLLO & CALLIOPE
|
ORPHEUS

✢ LETO ━━━━┓   ★ ZEUS

★ APOLLO ━━━━━━━┓   ✢ CALLIOPE

★ LINUS   ★ ORPHEUS ━━━━━━━ ✢ EURYDICE

★ god
✢ goddess
✳ man
✢ woman

ORPHIC MYSTERIES

[Gr]eco-Roman mystic cult, known as Orphism, was concerned with purification and the [after]life. Hymns and rhapsodies attributed to Orpheus were recited by the Orphics, who led [lives] of abstinence in the belief that their virtuousness would help free their souls from their [bodi]es when they entered the Underworld. A trial would condemn wrongdoers to punishment, [whil]e rewarding the righteous with new life. Thus liberated, the soul would be reincarnated in [a ne]w body.

realm of Hades, Orpheus wandered the world distraught. Some legends say that he killed himself; others say that grief led him to homosexuality, and that he was torn to pieces in a bacchanalian revel by Thracian women, jealous for his love. The only part of his body left intact was his head, which constantly cried out for Eurydice until the people of Lesbos buried it on their island.

IN LITERATURE AND MUSIC

The tales of Orpheus and Eurydice are favorite themes with dramatists and composers from many periods. The first great opera, composed by Monteverdi in 1607, was about the tragic couple; Haydn and Gluck also wrote operas about Orpheus; in 1858, Offenbach produced his famous opera *Orpheus in the Underworld*. In 1922, the poet Rilke wrote the *Sonnets to Orpheus* on the idea of communicating what is silent and uniting what is divided. In 1950, Jean Cocteau made a more off-beat film drama, *Orfée*.

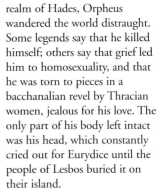

ORPHEUS AND EURYDICE
Orpheus, carrying his lyre, leads Eurydice out of the Underworld. Hades and Persephone look on.

ANCESTRY

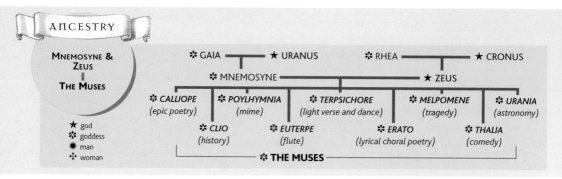

MNEMOSYNE & ZEUS
THE MUSES

✹ GAIA ──── ★ URANUS ✹ RHEA ──── ★ CRONUS

✹ MNEMOSYNE ──────────────── ★ ZEUS

★ god
✹ goddess
✸ man
✛ woman

✹ CALLIOPE	✹ POYLHYMNIA	✹ TERPSICHORE	✹ MELPOMENE	✹ URANIA
(epic poetry)	*(mime)*	*(light verse and dance)*	*(tragedy)*	*(astronomy)*

✹ CLIO	✹ EUTERPE	✹ ERATO	✹ THALIA
(history)	*(flute)*	*(lyrical choral poetry)*	*(comedy)*

✹ THE MUSES

THE MUSES

In Greek and Roman mythology, nine goddesses of the arts.

The Muses were the daughters of the Titaness Mnemosyne (Memory) and Zeus. They were the source of inspiration to artists, writers, and musicians.

Believed to be virgins living n the woods, sometimes near fountains, they were often depicted holding hands and dancing in a circle to symbolize the connection between the arts. The Muses embodied the highest intellectual and artistic endeavors of mankind, and their characteristics inspired people who, in turn, were obliged to acknowledge the Muses as the source of their creativity.

Calliope was the Muse of epic poetry, considered to be the most important of the arts.

Euterpe inspired lyric poetry and its accompanying music. Terpsichore helped dancers. Clio was Muse to historians whose talent for explaining the past was regarded as an art form in ancient Greece. Thalia was the Muse to comedians and those involved in festivals, which were spirited occasions if she was present. The sixth Muse, Melpomene, was more serious than the others and inspired tragedy in drama. Erato was Muse to amorous poetry; the Romans connected her with April, which was considered the month of lovers. Polyhymnia was associated with song and playing the lyre. The ninth Muse, Urania, was inspirer of astronomy, important to the

Greeks for its interpretive faculty in mythology and poetry.

Overseeing all the Muses was the Olympian god Apollo, who is represented in art in many periods, including Raphael's famous painting of Parnassus, the mountain near Delphi which was traditionally held sacred to Apollo and the Muses.

The most famous progeny of the Muses was Orpheus, son of the Thracian king Oeagrus and Calliope. After Apollo presented Orpheus with a lyre, the Muses taught him how to play it, compose lyrics, and sing. The result was said to be the best poetry and music the world has ever known.

GODDESSES OF THE ARTS
Apollo, Minerva, and the nine muses are shown, carrying symbols of their individual arts.

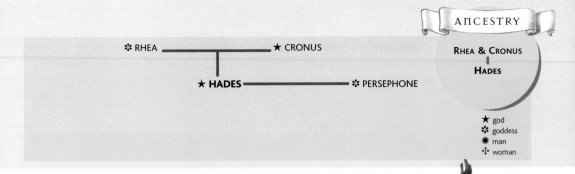

❋ RHEA ——————— ★ CRONUS

★ HADES ——————— ❋ PERSEPHONE

★ god
❋ goddess
✴ man
✛ woman

HADES/PLUTO

Ruler of the Underworld, called Hades in Greek myth and Pluto in Roman mythology.

When Zeus deposed his father Cronus, the three sons cast lots to divide the universe into three realms. Zeus won the sky, the second brother Poseidon was allotted the water, and Hades won the Underworld. The earth and Olympus, the mountain home of the gods in Thessaly, were shared by all three.

The ancient Greeks considered the name of Hades unlucky. The god of the dead was therefore usually referred to by other titles, among them Pluton (the rich one), Polydegmon (all-receiver), and Klymenos (the renowned). Despite being a grim and ruthless figure, Hades was never looked upon as an evil deity; neither was the "House of Hades," the Underworld, thought of as a hellish abode. Hades did not usually torment his inmates—the task of punishing wrongdoers was left to the Furies.

The dead arrived in the Underworld after being brought to the banks of the River Styx by Hermes. Then the spirits of the dead were ferried across the gray waters by the boatman Charon. The three-headed dog Cerberus ensured that no one fled back to the world of the living.

The main myth of Hades concerns Persephone. This daughter of Zeus and Demeter was exceptionally beautiful, so her mother kept her out of sight for fear of abduction. But Demeter did not expect such desire as Hades showed: the god simply emerged from beneath the earth and carried Persephone off in his chariot.

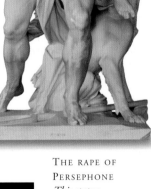

THE RAPE OF PERSEPHONE
This statue dramatically captures the moment when Hades abducted Persephone from a field.

TARTARUS, ABYSS OF THE UNDERWORLD

The souls of the most wicked were afflicted with eternal torment in Tartarus. This dreaded abyss of the Underworld was surrounded by walls and gates of bronze, and lay so deep in the earth that an anvil thrown down from heaven would take nine days to reach it. Among its inhabitants were Cronus, the Titans, Sisyphus, Ixion, and Tantalus.

TANTALUS

King of Lydia who offended the Greek gods and was punished for eternity in the abyss of Tartarus.

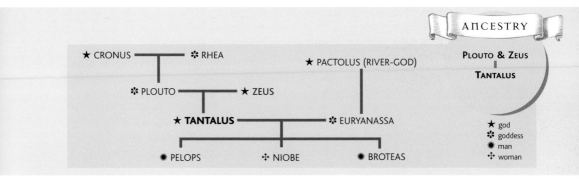

ANCESTRY

★ CRONUS — ❋ RHEA   ★ PACTOLUS (RIVER-GOD)   PLOUTO & ZEUS
                                                              │
❋ PLOUTO — ★ ZEUS   TANTALUS

        ★ TANTALUS — ❋ EURYANASSA

    ❋ PELOPS   ✣ NIOBE   ❋ BROTEAS

★ god
❋ goddess
❋ man
✣ woman

T his son of the Titaness Plouto, a daughter of Cronus and Rhea, and deity of wealth, became the rich ruler of Lydia (western Turkey). However, Tantalus commited a crime which the gods could never forgive, although the accounts of it vary. Some stories say he betrayed secrets entrusted to him by Zeus, his father; other legends say that he stole the food of the gods.

THE TORMENT OF TANTALUS
The fruit on the tree growing over Tantalus' head remained just out of reach, as did the water in which he stood chin-deep.

The best-known account describes his attempted deception of the gods by serving them a dish of human flesh.

Having invited the Olympian gods to a banquet, Tantalus discovered that he did not have enough food to offer them and, either to test the gods or simply as a gesture of good will, he included a course prepared from the dissected body of his son Pelops. The fare was recognized by all the divine guests, except Demeter, who was lost in thought about her missing daughter Persephone. Hermes fetched the soul of Pelops back

from the Underworld and the gods restored him to life. Because Demeter had absentmindedly eaten part of Pelops' shoulder, she produced an ivory replacement for him.

In punishment for offending the gods, Tantalus was imprisoned in Tartarus. Here he was kept perpetually hungry and thirsty while standing chin-deep in water with fruit hanging from branches just above his head. Whenever he tried to drink the water or eat the fruit, they receded just beyond his reach—hence the word "tantalize."

SISYPHUS

Another figure condemned by the gods to eternal torment in Tartarus was Sisyphus, founder of Corinth and in some myths regarded as father of Odysseus. Once, the river-god Asopus went to the city in search of his daughter who had been abducted by Zeus. Knowing of her whereabouts, Sisyphus told Asopus on condition that he would supply his citadel with a perennial spring. That agreed, Asopus looked to take revenge on Zeus who, in turn, was furious with Sisyphus for betraying godly secrets. The god punished Sisyphus by making him roll a boulder continually uphill. Each time he nearly reached the top, his strength would fail, and the boulder would roll downhill.

AN UPHILL STRUGGLE
On this 4th-century BC Greek vase, Sisyphus is shown pushing his boulder uphill. In this version, there is a god or goddess pushing down on the boulder.

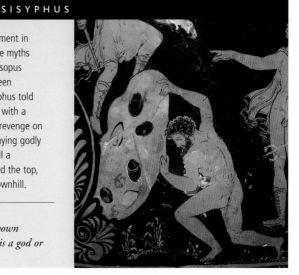

DIONYSUS/BACCHUS

*Greek God of wine and ecstasy, whose cult promised
individual salvation; Bacchus was the Roman counterpart.*

BACCHUS AND ARIADNE
*Bacchus emerges with his followers
from the landscape on the right.
Falling in love with Ariadne on
sight, he leaps from his chariot,
drawn by two cheetahs, toward her.
She is fearful at first, but he raised
her to heaven and turned her into a
constellation, represented by the stars
above her head.*

Woodland spirits
usually accompanied
Dionysus. Of these,
the Sileni were hairy men with
horse's ears, who were wise but
very drunken; the satyrs were
horse- or goatlike men who were
lustful and also very drunken.
These rowdy followers protected
fertility, a circumstance which

suggests that Dionysus may once,
like Demeter, have been a deity
of vegetation and agriculture.
His human followers were
women known as Maenads
("frenzied ones").

According to one tradition,
Dionysus was conceived at the
city of Thebes, where his mother
Semele was a princess. This

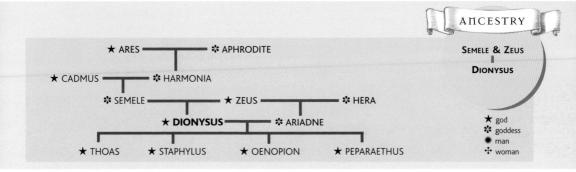

SEMELE & ZEUS
|
DIONYSUS

★ ARES ——— ❖ APHRODITE

★ CADMUS ——— ❖ HARMONIA

❖ SEMELE ——— ★ ZEUS ——— ❖ HERA

★ DIONYSUS ——— ❖ ARIADNE

★ THOAS   ★ STAPHYLUS   ❖ OENOPION   ★ PEPARAETHUS

★ god
❖ goddess
✳ man
✢ woman

daughter of Cadmus, the city's founder, was loved by Zeus, who disguised himself as a man. When Zeus' wife Hera heard about the liaison and then discovered that Semele was pregnant by Zeus, she could hardly control her jealous rage and devised a terrible but subtle act of revenge on both parties.

Hera disguised herself as Semele's old nurse and persuaded the princess to demand proof from Zeus that he really was a god by appearing to her in his true form. To do this, Semele persuaded Zeus to grant her the favor of seeing him in his true glory; but the god's brightness was so intense that it shriveled Semele to nothing. Zeus managed to save the fetus of Dionysus from Semele's womb by sewing him into his thigh where the unborn child stayed for several months until he was ready to enter the world.

SON OF PERSEPHONE

A tradition from Orphic mystery religion gives a different account of Dionysus' life, making him the son of Persephone, queen of the Underworld. Dionysus came to Thebes as a young man, but King Pentheus refused to recognize his right to be worshiped and imprisoned the god of wine for carousing with the local women. No jail could hold Dionysus, and reports of wild revels in the town reached the king. Pentheus spied on their rituals from a tree, but he was seen and, being mistaken for a lion, the unfortunate ruler was torn limb from limb.

BACCHANALIAN REVELS

The cult of Dionysus was famous for its orgiastic revelries. Dancing, singing, and drunken shouting easily spiraled out of control in a frenzy of joy. Despite its image of hedonistic indulgence, there was a religious purpose to these ritual practices. It was believed that by drinking excessive amounts of wine, members of the cult could shed their social inhibitions and become liberated in a realm of divine abandonment. Public festivals, known as the Bacchanalia, involved people dressing up as characters from the myths. In Euripides' play *Bacchae*, the rituals are extreme: animals are dismembered and naked priestesses perform indecent acts amid scenes of debauchery.

THE MIDAS TOUCH

A son of the fertility goddess Cybele (from a Roman mystery cult) was the legendary King Midas of Phrygia, a land fabled for its wealth. The most famous story about Midas concerns his ability to find wealth, a gift still referred to as the "Midas touch." He once pleased Dionysus by returning the god's horselike companion Silenus to him after he had been captured drunk by country folk. Dionysus was so grateful that he offered Midas whatever he wished. Without hesitation, Midas asked Dionysus to allow everything he touched to be turned to gold. At first, Midas was delighted with his wish, but his joy soon turned to horror when he discovered that his food turned to gold whenever he took a bite. Dionysus took pity on him and sent him to cleanse himself in a river, the silt of which thereafter contained gold dust. Phrygia was known to be a rich region, being one of the first to mint gold coins for the Greeks.

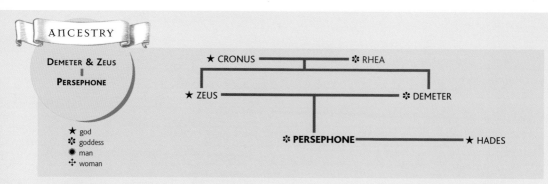

DEMETER & ZEUS
|
PERSEPHONE

★ god
✽ goddess
● man
✧ woman

★ CRONUS ━━━━━━━ ✽ RHEA

★ ZEUS ━━━━━━━━━━━━━━━━━━ ✽ DEMETER

✽ PERSEPHONE ━━━━━━━━━ ★ HADES

PERSEPHONE

Queen of the Underworld and wife of Hades.

Persephone was the exceptionally beautiful daughter of Zeus and his sister Demeter, goddess of vegetation. To keep her safe, Demeter hid Persephone in Sicily, but Hades, god of the Underworld, discovered her. Seeing Persephone walking in the woods with her maids, Hades decided to abduct her. With the permission of his brother Zeus, he rose in his chariot from the earth, snatched her, then quickly disappeared beneath the ground again.

While the grief-stricken Demeter searched the earth for her lost daughter, Persephone pined away in Hades' gloomy kingdom. Although she refused all food, she inadvertently ate some pomegranate seeds Hades offered her in order to bind her to his realm. Zeus was obliged to reach a compromise with Demeter, who had threatened to destroy mankind if she did not see her daughter again. They agreed that Persephone would spend one half of the year with her husband and the other half with her mother.

Persephone accepted the role decreed by Zeus and was therefore worshiped as the goddess of birth and death. As Kore (the virgin), Persephone was said to be the power of growth within the seed-corn buried in pits during the summer months before the autumn sowing.

The myth has an obvious parallel with that of Aphrodite and Adonis, in which story a quarrel between Aphrodite and Persephone was resolved by allowing Adonis to spend some of the year with his mother and some of the time with his admirer Persephone.

PERSEPHONE
A 5th-century BC Greek silver decadrachma coin with the head of the goddess Persephone.

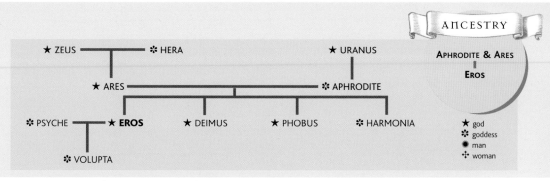

ANCESTRY

APHRODITE & ARES

EROS

★ ZEUS ——— ❋ HERA

★ URANUS

★ ARES ————————————— ❋ APHRODITE

❋ PSYCHE ——— ★ **EROS**   ★ DEIMUS   ★ PHOBUS   ❋ HARMONIA

❋ VOLUPTA

★ god
❋ goddess
☀ man
✣ woman

EROS / CUPID

Youthful god of love in Greek mythology; the Roman god
Cupid (Desire) or Amor (Love).

Some traditions say that Eros originally hatched from a primal world egg and came into the universe as the power of passion. As such, he was considered to be the first of the gods, without whom none of the others could have come into existence. Eros was a double-sexed being with golden wings and four heads who consorted with Night, and everything on earth and in heaven derived from their union.

CUPID'S ANTICS

As later mythology tended to revolve around the Olympian gods, this primeval power of passion was believed to be a son of Aphrodite (the Olympian goddess of love) and Ares. Eros became the masculine ideal of love, while Aphrodite represented the feminine side. In time, as Zeus' power rose in the pantheon, he gained more control of Aphrodite, and her son suffered in status as a result.

When the Romans adopted the Greek myths, Eros was further emasculated to become the familiar winged figure of Cupid, the angelic infant who shoots arrows of love into people's hearts. In Renaissance art, he is depicted as a chubby child because he was playful in a mischievous and charming way, although the effects of his actions could be anything but childlike, his barbed arrows setting hearts on fire without warning or design.

BELOVED PSYCHE

Eros loved a beautiful maiden named Psyche. Since Eros was immortal, he forbade Psyche to look at him or even to know his identity. Overcome with curiosity, one night she took a lamp to bed and gazed at the sleeping Eros. Startled at the sight of the beautiful young god, she woke him accidentally. Eros rose quickly and flew away.

Psyche went in search of her lover, without success. She ended up at the palace of Aphrodite, who enslaved her and set her impossible tasks. Finally, she was discovered by Eros, who took her to Olympus. There they were reunited and their marriage was celebrated by the gods.

PSYCHE REVIVED BY THE KISS OF EROS
A beautiful marble statue by Canova, depicting their true love.

PANDORA

Created by Zeus, this beautiful woman unleashed evil on to the world.

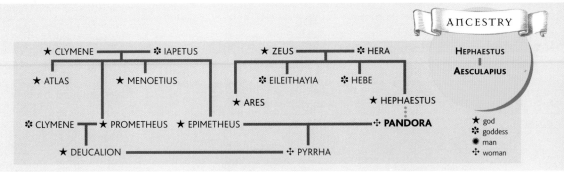

★ CLYMENE ——— ❖ IAPETUS   ★ ZEUS ——— ❖ HERA   **HEPHAESTUS**

AESCULAPIUS

★ ATLAS   ★ MENOETIUS   ❖ EILEITHAYIA   ❖ HEBE

★ ARES   ★ HEPHAESTUS

❖ CLYMENE ——★ PROMETHEUS   ★ EPIMETHEUS ———————— ❖ **PANDORA**

★ DEUCALION ———————————————— ❖ PYRRHA

★ god
❖ goddess
✹ man
✛ woman

Whereas Zeus had a stern attitude to people and harassed them, Prometheus the Titan was kind towards them and offered what protection he could. Hostility between the two gods began after Prometheus had created the first men on earth. Their enmity was compounded when Prometheus returned to men the gift of fire which Zeus in his anger had taken away from them. Zeus was so incensed at Prometheus' action that he decided to punish mankind by creating Pandora, who would plague the world with evils.

PANDORA'S BOX
Compelled to open the box the gods had given her, she let out all the evils of the world. Only hope remained.

Zeus instructed the smith god Hephaestus to make Pandora out of clay. Athena breathed life into her and Aphrodite gave her beauty. She was taught guile by the quick-witted Hermes who also arranged her marriage to Prometheus' gullible brother Epimetheus. Prometheus (meaning "forethought") gave Epithemeus (meaning "afterthought") dire warnings to avoid Pandora, but he ignored them and married her; furthermore, Epimetheus accepted as her dowry a sealed jar of divine gifts. Little did the couple know that the jar contained all the evils that could beset the world. One version of the myth says that Prometheus knew the contents of the jar because he had painstakingly filled it with the world's woes:

sickness, labor, vice, madness, old age. The only good thing in it was hope, which lay at the bottom of the jar. One day, against her husband's advice, Pandora opened the jar out of curiosity and released evil into the world. Hence, the term "Pandora's Box" has come to mean a source of great strife.

According to another version of the story, the jar contained everything that was good, and when the lid was raised, everything virtuous escaped.

Pandora's daughter Pyrrha married Deucalion, the Greek equivalent of the biblical character Noah. When Zeus determined to destroy mankind because of its wickedness, Deucalion and Pyrrha survived the great flood he sent by building a boat and stocking it with food.

THE GREEK EVE

Just as Eve was presented in the Bible as the source of evil in the world, so in Hesiod's *Theogony* Pandora is her equivalent in Greek literature. Accordingly, Zeus punished mankind by creating women, the first of whom was Pandora, married to the gullible Epimetheus. Pandora's metaphorical box of strife bears some similarities with Adam and Eve's fall from grace when they were punished with everlasting toil and pain. It is likely that Pandora, literally meaning "all gifts," was originally a pre-Greek earth goddess.

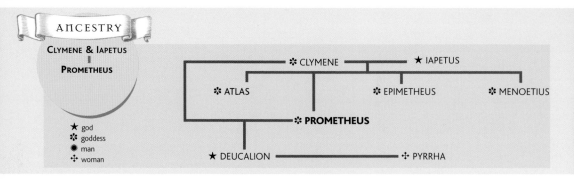

ANCESTRY chart:
- ❋ CLYMENE — ★ IAPETUS
- ❋ ATLAS — ❋ EPIMETHEUS — ❋ MENOETIUS
- ❋ PROMETHEUS
- ★ DEUCALION — ✦ PYRRHA

PROMETHEUS

God of fire and craftsmen, punished by Zeus for his kindness to humanity.

Although Prometheus helped Zeus overthrow his father Cronus, he later rebelled against the king of the gods because Zeus was hostile toward people. Prometheus was both a fire god and a master of many skills. According to one tradition, it was he who made the first men out of clay. He instructed them in various arts, including architecture, astronomy, navigation, and medicine.

But Zeus, growing angry at their increasing powers, wished to destroy mankind. When Prometheus tricked Zeus by arranging with humans for the god to receive only the poor entrails of their sacrifice, not the tasty meat, Zeus was enraged when he realized he had been duped. In response, Zeus hid fire from mankind to prevent them from eating cooked meat, but Prometheus then stole it back and gave fire back to mankind. As a punishment for stealing the fire, Zeus swore a twofold revenge. He ordered Hephaestus to make a clay woman who would plague mankind. Her name was Pandora. Secondly, Prometheus was chained to a rock on Mount Caucasus and each day an eagle came to devour his liver. Since he was immortal, however, Prometheus' liver regrew each night.

Prometheus, whose name means "forethought," was able to see into the future. He warned his brother Epimetheus not to marry Pandora, whose dowry would eventually unleash evil onto the world. And when Prometheus forewarned Zeus that Thetis' son Achilles was destined to be his rival, Zeus released him from bondage in gratitude, ordering Heracles to shoot the eagle and break the god's binding chains.

Prometheus' son Deucalion saved mankind from a flood loosed on the world by Zeus, a story which has its parallel in the biblical story of Noah.

IN LITERATURE

The Greek dramatist Aeschylus was the likely author of *Prometheus Bound*, in which the protagonist is extolled as the champion of man against the new Olympian authority. The play is part of a trilogy in which Heracles frees Prometheus from bondage. This theme was developed by the English poet Percy Bysshe Shelley in his lyrical drama *Prometheus Unbound* (1819). He portrayed Prometheus as one whose knowledge would bring an enlightened realm of freedom and love, instead of the Olympian reality of hatred and oppression.

As the suffering creator of man and a free thinker, Prometheus has appealed to various writers. The early fathers of the Christian Church found in him a ready symbol of the Passion of Christ. Lord Byron identified with his spirit of fighting for freedom, and Goethe also stressed Prometheus' sympathy with the suffering of mankind. Shelley's wife Mary developed the theme in a gothic horror fantasy in her novel *Frankenstein, or the Modern Prometheus* in 1819.

PROMETHEUS BOUND
Oil paining by Titian, showing Prometheus being punished by having his liver pecked by an eagle.

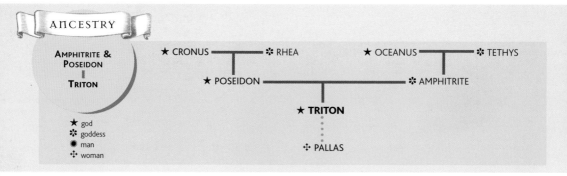

AMPHITRITE &
POSEIDON
|
TRITON

★ god
❋ goddess
✹ man
✣ woman

★ CRONUS ─┬─ ❋ RHEA   ★ OCEANUS ─┬─ ❋ TETHYS

★ POSEIDON ────────────────── ❋ AMPHITRITE

★ TRITON

✣ PALLAS

TRITON

Merman of Greek mythology, son of Poseidon, responsible for calming storms.

This immortal creature had the head and torso of a man, and the fins and tail of a fish or dolphin. Triton's name may be a derivation of Amphitrite, his mother, who ruled the sea as a moon-goddess. As Amphitrite's son, Triton was associated with the lucky new moon. In Greek mythology, whenever Triton wished to calm the waves, he would blow on a conch shell; likewise, in the Roman poet Ovid's myth of the flood, Neptune commanded Triton to blow his conch shell to push back the waters, a feature of classical mythology that is well represented in fountain statues of Triton in baroque art. Triton's depiction as a dolphin is linked to calm seas, when the creatures were most likely to appear.

MOODY CREATURE

The merman would rescue ships in distress, but, equally, he could cause their sinking. In Virgil's epic story of the *Aeneid*, Triton drowned Misenus for challenging the gods with music from his horn. In the story of Jason and the Argonauts, when Euphemus asked Triton for directions to the Mediterranean Sea, the nonchalant merman offered no more than a finger pointed towards a river. Later, in a change of heart, the sea-god gave Euphemus a clod of earth to symbolize sovereignty for his descendants over Libya (which the Greeks colonized). When Euphemus sacrificed a sheep in

thanks, Triton hauled the *Argo* by its keel through the water all the way to the Mediterranean. A foster-daughter of Triton, Pallas (unrelated to Styx's husband), was accidentally killed while sparring with her playmate, the goddess Athena, who then adopted her name in grief and became known as Pallas Athena.

TRIUMPH OF GALATEA
The merman Triton rescues the Nereid Galatea at sea.

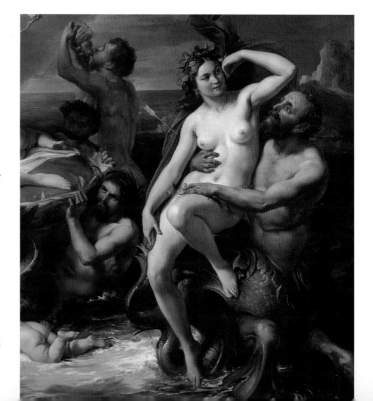

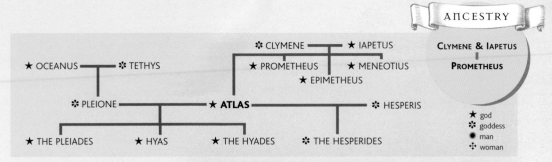

ANCESTRY

CLYMENE & IAPETUS

PROMETHEUS

✷ CLYMENE ── ★ IAPETUS

★ OCEANUS ─── ✷ TETHYS ★ PROMETHEUS ── ★ MENEOTIUS

★ EPIMETHEUS

✷ PLEIONE ──── ★ **ATLAS** ──── ✷ HESPERIS

★ THE PLEIADES   ★ HYAS   ★ THE HYADES   ✷ THE HESPERIDES

★ god
✷ goddess
✦ man
✧ woman

ATLAS

A Titan who bore the sky on his shoulders.

Originally Atlas was known as the guardian of the pillars that supported the heavens, but later he was associated with holding up the sky itself. He was most famous for the part he played in the Titanomachy, a ten-year struggle between the Titans and the Olympian gods. Atlas became leader of the Titans when Cronus grew battle-weary. Despite Atlas' best efforts at rallying his forces, they proved no match for the Olympians, led by Zeus, whose superior arsenal and monster power eventually overwhelmed the old gods. Atlas' brother Menoetius was struck by a thunderbolt in battle and descended to Tartarus. Most of the Titans who survived were cast into the abyss of Tartarus, where they were guarded by the Hecatoncheires, hundred-handed monsters.

As their military leader, Atlas was given the more severe punishment of having to support the heavens on his shoulders forever. This myth explained to the Greeks why the sky did not

fall on the earth. One legend says that the range of mountains in North Africa bearing his name was created when Atlas was turned to stone after Perseus showed him the Gorgon Medusa's head. This proved a blessing in disguise, since Atlas was thereafter strong enough to support the heavens.

APPLES OF THE HESPERIDES

On his eleventh labor, Heracles was told by King Eurystheus to fetch three apples from Hera's golden apple tree growing in an orchard on the slopes of Mount Atlas. Care of the tree was entrusted to Atlas' three daughters, the Hesperides. When Hera discovered that the girls had betrayed that trust and were stealing the apples, she put Ladon, a vigilant dragon, in

THE WEIGHT OF THE WORLD ON HIS SHOULDERS
Atlas is shown supporting the heavens on his shoulders.

charge. Heracles was advised not to pluck the fruit himself, but to ask Atlas to do it for him. On finding the wondrous orchard, Heracles shot Ladon with an arrow and offered to hold up the world while the Titan plucked the apples. Atlas was so pleased to be relieved of his burden for an hour that he pleaded with Heracles to allow him to deliver the apples to Eurystheus himself. Heracles agreed, but tricked Atlas by asking him to carry the load for a moment while he put a pad on his head. When the gullible Atlas took the burden, Heracles picked up the three apples and walked away.

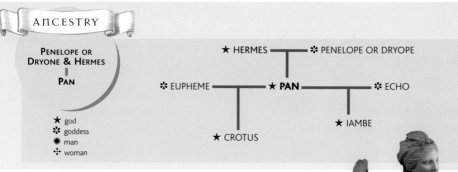

ANCESTRY

PENELOPE OR
DRYONE & HERMES
|
PAN

★ HERMES ——— ❋ PENELOPE OR DRYOPE

❋ EUPHEME ——— ★ PAN ——— ❋ ECHO

★ IAMBE

★ CROTUS

★ god
❋ goddess
✴ man
✣ woman

PAN

*Greek god of the pastures,
protector of sheep and goats.*

This favorite of Dionysus was a mischievous god born with the horns and legs of a goat. His mother, who may have been Penelope, wife of Odysseus, was so shocked by his appearance at birth that she took flight, leaving her offspring to be raised by nymphs. Pan's father, possibly Hermes, then took him to Olympus for the gods' amusement.

One meaning of Pan is "feeder," which alludes to the god's pastoral care. He was also responsible for the fertility of herds and flocks. His own wantonness was legendary; he was particularly attracted to nymphs, including Echo, whom some said he struck dumb except for the ability to repeat herself, since she did not return his love. One nymph, Syrinx, changed herself into a clump of reeds to escape his clutches. In revenge, Pan chopped down several reeds and made them into a musical instrument called a syrinx, or pan pipes. He played wonderful tunes on the pipes, beguiling both nymphs and women, such as the moon-goddess Selene, whom he tried to seduce with the gift of a fine fleece.

Although Pan was usually playful, an irritable streak in his character could quickly disrupt rural tranquility. The god easily inspired a sudden inexplicable fright in both animals and men—hence the word "panic." He could cause stampedes in the heat of the day or frightening dreams at night. When Zeus overthrew his tyrannical father Cronus, Pan helped him in the act by creating confusion with blasts on his conch shell.

IN LITERATURE

From classical times to the modern day, Pan has been the patron of pastoral poets. His birthplace, Arcadia, has been idealized as an idyllic place, largely on his account. In Shelley's "Hymn to Pan" and Keats' "Endymion," Pan is seen as the god of wild nature. The sixteenth-century French writer

APHRODITE OF THE SANDAL
Group statue showing Aphrodite, Pan and Eros. There is no known myth to accompany this statue.

François Rabelais identified Pan with the Good Shepherd of the Gospels and some philosophers associated the wild commotion of his character with the soul's irrational element. Pan's common appearance in art alongside Venus and Cupid, both gods of love, is thought to imply the dictum "love conquers all," since *pan* in Greek means "all."

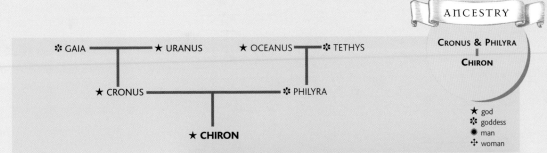

❀ GAIA ——————— ★ URANUS   ★ OCEANUS ——— ❀ TETHYS

★ CRONUS ———————————————— ❀ PHILYRA

★ CHIRON

★ god
❀ goddess
✳ man
✣ woman

CHIRON

A leading figure among the centaurs, an immortal half-human, half-horse; sage, prophet, teacher, and healer.

CHIRON AND ACHILLES
Wise Chiron was tutor to many Greek heros, including Achilles.

Chiron was unusual among the centaurs because he did not lead an indulgent lifestyle of chaotic drinking and carousing (most centaurs were notorious for their violence and vulgarity when they were drunk). By contrast, Chiron was known for his wisdom and good behavior. He was tutor to many Greek heroes, including Heracles, Achilles, Theseus, and Jason, with the ability to enable his pupils to reach their highest potential and discover their true destiny. He was also an astrologer who could read a person's fate in the stars.

Chiron was conceived when Cronus took the form of a horse and coupled with the nymph Philyra, which accounts for his different ancestry from the other centaurs. As a child of Cronus, Chiron was immortal, but he nobly sacrificed his immortality after being wounded in a skirmish. This happened when his former pupil Heracles was

dining with his friend Pholus in a cave; vapors from their wine wafted outside and intoxicated a bevy of centaurs gathered there. Driven wild by the heady fumes, the centaurs attacked the cave with rocks and branches, while Heracles fought back by shooting arrows poisoned with Hydra's blood. During the conflict, an arrow struck Chiron by mistake. Although he was a master of herbal medicine, the man-horse was unable to heal

himself. His agony prompted Prometheus to appeal to Zeus to shed Chiron's immortality so that he could die. Zeus agreed. As a token of respect for Chiron, Zeus gave the honorable centaur pride of place in the heavens by setting him as the constellation Sagittarius.

PART II
HEROES

In this section about the adventures and misadventures of the mortals, the mythology of ancient Greece has reached its most developed stage. Elaborate tales of heroic deeds and tragedies unfold. Their characters are human or semi-divine, and engage our sympathies, yet they are pitched into dreamlike landscapes where the gods intervene and subject these creatures of destiny to the toughest of examinations.

Six cycles of legends are covered by chapter, each one relating to a royal house based at one of the main Greek centers. Although adventures took their heroes beyond the shores of Greece, most dynastic rulers were rooted on the mainland. The exceptions were Crete, home to the great Minoan civilization, with its strong connections to Mycenae, and Troy, the fabled doomed city in Asia Minor. So entangled were the fortunes of the Greeks with their former enemy that the destruction of Troy had come to represent the culmination of their collective mythology.

Ingenuity, skill, and fortune all play their part in these legends that have evolved over the centuries. Many of the myths have a moral to their story, but others equally appear to be unfair until divine intervention restores the balance of justice. Notions of fate and justice lie at the heart of these sagas that toss their subjects about like flotsam in a squall. As different myth-tellers lend their own slant to a legend, so traditions have come to vary in their details of the same story. Thus, the Homeric account differs from the Orphic one, which differs again from the Olympian version. Part of the reason for this disparity is the relative value placed on the myth concerned. Each will mean something different to each reader. The strong storylines make them memorable, but people's feelings in response to the events described, and the impacts on the characters involved, will vary from one reader to another.

And so it is that modern versions of these myths, dramatized for modern audiences, have developed new interpretations of the characters involved. Avant-garde artists have created fresh visions and turned stereotypes on their head. Whoever in classical Greece, for example, would have thought of Picasso's dyspeptic Minotaur lounging in harmony with a reclining woman?

JASON

AND THE

ARGONAUTS

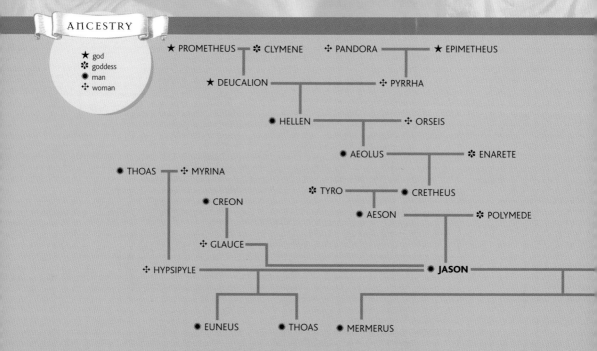

★ PROMETHEUS — ❋ CLYMENE   ✧ PANDORA — ★ EPIMETHEUS

★ DEUCALION — ✧ PYRRHA

✵ HELLEN — ✧ ORSEIS

✵ AEOLUS — ❋ ENARETE

❋ TYRO — ✵ CRETHEUS

✵ THOAS — ✧ MYRINA

✵ CREON

✵ AESON — ❋ POLYMEDE

✧ GLAUCE

✧ HYPSIPYLE — ✵ **JASON**

✵ EUNEUS   ✵ THOAS   ✵ MERMERUS

T his chapter is the first of the cycles of legendary
heroes and involves Jason's fabled quest to recover
the Golden Fleece from Colchis. Reared by wise Chiron,
the beast that was half-horse, half-man, Jason assembled
fifty men, the Argonauts, for the great voyage on the Argo.
He married Medea and had numerous adventures on the
way to Iolcus. But he fell out of favor with the gods and
wandered as an outcast until his old age, when the prow of
the old ship collapsed and killed him.

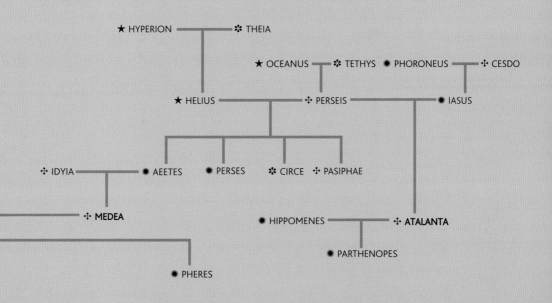

JASON

Legendary Greek hero and leader of the Argonauts.

Jason was usually understood to be a prince from Thessalia whose father had been dethroned. Fearing for her son's safety, Jason's mother sent him secretly to the cave of the centaur Chiron. This wise horse-man tutored many of the greatest figures in Greek mythology, including Aesculapius and Achilles. The crew that Jason eventually took in quest of the Golden Fleece included several of Chiron's pupils.

JASON'S QUEST

The quest for the Golden Fleece occurred almost by accident. Jason had returned home to the city of Iolcus and claimed his father's throne, but because it was a festival day the usurper Pelias was unable to kill the young contender. Not only would his death have transgressed the laws of hospitality, but the gods might also have taken grave offense at this violation of their worship. So Pelias pretended to step down in Jason's favor in return for the marvelous Golden Fleece of a ram, which hung from a tree in Colchis (in Crimea) and was guarded by a dragon.

With the support of the Delphic Oracle and the goddess Hera, Jason gathered his band of Argonauts, including the great hero Heracles. After a strenuous voyage, which included a stop at Lemnos where Jason lay with Hypsipyle, producing two children, they reached Colchis. With the aid of a local princess, Medea, whom Jason married, the fleece was eventually found. When their ship, the *Argo*, hastened away with the prize, pursued by the inhabitants of Colchis, Medea suggested that

THE GOLDEN FLEECE

Athamas, king of Boeotia, vowed to kill his son Phryxus for allegedly bringing famine to the land. However, the gods decided that Phryxus' life should be spared, and, just as Athamas was about to strike the fatal blow, a magical ram with a golden fleece appeared. The ram told Phryxus and his sister Helle to climb on his back and immediately it flew with them away to Colchis. Helle fell into the sea on the way, at the place since known as the Hellespont or the Dardanelles. At Colchis, Phryxus was welcomed by King Aeetes; he then sacrificed the ram to Zeus and hung the fleece in the grove of the god Ares.

they should cut up her brother Apsyrtus and throw him overboard to slow down the vessels chasing them. The Argonauts did this, forcing their pursuers to gather up the remains for a decent burial.

Medea's interest in dismemberment could also have helped Jason on his return to Iolcus, since she tricked the daughters of the usurper Pelias into cutting up and boiling their father in the belief that they could restore his youth. Most versions of this myth suggest that Jason never became king, but instead retired voluntarily to the Peloponnese.

The goddess Aphrodite was said to have been responsible for making Medea fall violently in love with Jason. Aphrodite's purpose was to harm Pelias, whom she hated. The magical skills of Medea were therefore put at Jason's disposal, allowing him to perform the herculean labors necessary to win the Golden Fleece. Medea in Greek means "the cunning one," and she was certainly associated with sorcery.

JASON RETURNS TO PELIAS
Jason is shown taking the Golden Fleece back to Pelias in order to claim his kingdom.

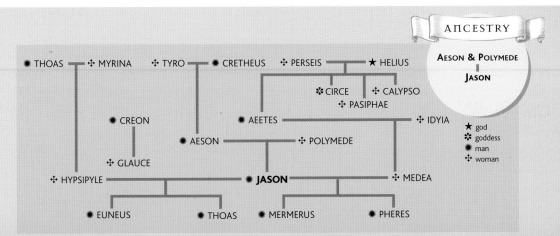

ANCESTRY

AESON & POLYMEDE

JASON

* THOAS — ✤ MYRINA   ✤ TYRO — * CRETHEUS   ✤ PERSEIS — ★ HELIUS

❋ CIRCE — ✤ CALYPSO

✤ PASIPHAE

* CREON   * AEETES — ✤ IDYIA

* AESON — ✤ POLYMEDE

✤ GLAUCE

★ god
❋ goddess
* man
✤ woman

✤ HYPSIPYLE — **JASON** — ✤ MEDEA

* EUNEUS   * THOAS   * MERMERUS   * PHERES

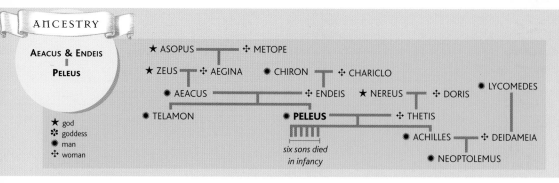

ANCESTRY

ANCESTRY

AEACUS & ENDEIS
|
PELEUS

★ ASOPUS ——— ✢ METOPE

★ ZEUS — ✢ AEGINA   ✳ CHIRON — ✢ CHARICLO

✳ AEACUS ————— ✢ ENDEIS   ★ NEREUS — ✢ DORIS   ✳ LYCOMEDES

✳ TELAMON   **✳ PELEUS** ——— ✢ THETIS

six sons died
in infancy   ✳ ACHILLES — ✢ DEIDAMEIA

✳ NEOPTOLEMUS

★ god
✳ goddess
✳ man
✢ woman

PELEUS

An Argonaut and son of Aeacus, king of Aegina.

Peleus of Iolcus was husband of the sea nymph Thetis. It was at their wedding feast that the three goddesses—Athena, Hera, and Aphrodite—all claimed a golden apple addressed to "the fairest of them all." Paris, the handsomest man, judged the most beautiful goddess to be Aphrodite.

Peleus was one of the brave men of Greece who answered a call to take part in a great boar hunt in Calydon. The goddess Artemis had sent the wild animal to rampage among cattle belonging to King Oeneus as a punishment for not making his yearly sacrifices to the Olympian gods. The hunters, among them Jason and Nestor, attacked their quarry armed with bows and arrows, spears, and axes. Peleus fought boldly, but accidentally killed fellow hunter Eurytion with a javelin aimed at the boar.

Peleus numbered among the volunteers who helped Heracles in his ninth labor to fetch the golden girdle of Ares worn by the Amazonian queen Hippolyta. He also sailed with Heracles in his war fleet to Troy, during which campaign Heracles burned the city and put Priam on the Trojan throne as an ally.

A misunderstanding arose between Peleus and his wife when she was attempting to make their son Achilles immortal by the use of fire. As a result, Thetis left Peleus and returned to her homeland, the sea. Uncertain about his own ability as a parent, Peleus entrusted the upbringing of Achilles to the centaur Chiron. When Achilles died during the Trojan War, Thetis returned to console the distraught Peleus and took him to live with her at sea.

THETIS CARRIED OFF BY
PELEUS
*An engraving from a Greek
vase found on Rhodes.*

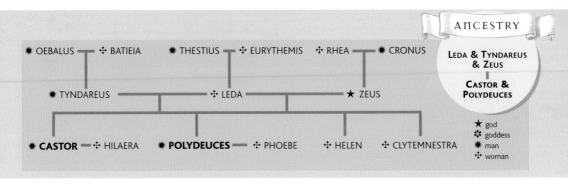

OEBALUS — BATIEIA THESTIUS — EURYTHEMIS RHEA — CRONUS

TYNDAREUS ——— LEDA ——— ZEUS

CASTOR — HILAERA POLYDEUCES — PHOEBE HELEN CLYTEMNESTRA

CASTOR AND POLYDEUCES

In Greek mythology, Castor and Polydeuces were heavenly twins and brothers of Helen of Troy; the Romans knew them by their more familiar names of Castor and Pollux.

THE DIOSCURI
A c. 6th-century BC stone carving of the twins and their horses.

These twins were thought to have been born either in Sparta or in heaven after Zeus, in the form of a swan, had seduced the beautiful Leda. She produced two eggs, one containing Castor and Polydeuces, and a second bearing Helen and her sister Clytemnestra. Another tradition holds that Leda's husband, the Spartan king Tyndareus, lay with Leda on the same night and that Castor was his son, while Polydeuces was born of Zeus.

Known also as the Dioscuri ("sons of Zeus"), the twin brothers traveled with Jason and the Argonauts in quest of the Golden Fleece, and helped Jason campaign against his enemies at home when the voyagers returned. They became renowned athletes—Castor for his horsemanship and Polydeuces for

his boxing. They were involved, too, in the rescue of their sister Helen after Theseus had carried her off to Attica.

The most famous exploit of the twins was an attempted abduction. They aspired to marry their cousins, Phoebe and Hilaera, who were already betrothed to the princes Idas and Lynceus. Nevertheless, Castor and Polydeuces carried them off to Sparta, sparking a bitter feud. In the final confrontation, Idas and Lynceus were slain and Castor received a fatal spear wound.

The tradition that believed Castor to be the mortal son of Tyndareus tells of Polydeuces' grief at his half-brother's death.

He was said to be so distraught that he offered to share his immortality with him. Zeus took pity on them both and agreed that Castor should spend alternately one day in the Underworld and one day in Olympus with the gods. Their place among the stars is symbolized by the constellation Gemini, Latin for "twins."

The Romans were great devotees of the twins. They believed that these divine heroes aided them on the battlefield.

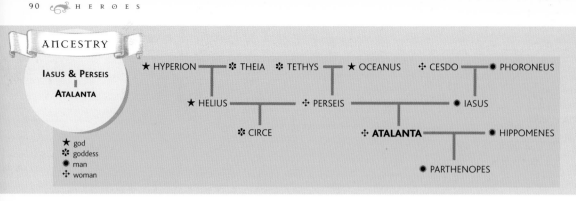

ANCESTRY

IASUS & PERSEIS
|
ATALANTA

★ HYPERION ── ❋ THEIA   ❋ TETHYS ── ★ OCEANUS   ✧ CESDO ── ❋ PHORONEUS

★ HELIUS ──── ✧ PERSEIS ──── ❋ IASUS

❋ CIRCE

✧ **ATALANTA** ──── ❋ HIPPOMENES

❋ PARTHENOPES

★ god
❋ goddess
❋ man
✧ woman

ATALANTA

A huntress in Greek mythology who was renowned, like Artemis, for her speed and daring.

Atalanta was the only daughter of Iasus and Perseis. Her father, who had inherited a portion of the Peloponnese from his father, King Phoroneus, wanted a son and heir, and was so disappointed by the birth of a daughter that he abandoned her as a baby on a hillside. Luckily, Artemis sent a she-bear to suckle the infant, and she was brought up by a band of hunters who taught her their skills.

THE HUNTING PARTY
Atalanta figured among hunters, including Castor and Polydeuces, who took part in the great Calydonian boar hunt. Armed with a bow and arrow, Atalanta took up a position on the far flank of the hunting party. Where others failed to hit the beast, some even falling prey to its ferocious tusks, Atalanta was the first hunter to strike a hit, lodging an arrow behind the boar's ear. However, this seemed only to enrage the animal. It then rushed at Theseus, who

missed hitting the creature with his spear and would have perished had not Meleager, the finest javelin-thrower in all of Greece, mortally wounded the beast just in time. Meleager had, in fact, fallen in love with Atalanta, and when he was awarded the boar's pelt for his exceptional skill, he insisted on presenting it to his beloved whose arrow had drawn the first blood.

VIRGIN LEOPARDS
Having been warned by an oracle that marriage would bring unhappiness, Atalanta remained a virgin, and for sport made her suitors race against her,

---

BEAR HUNT
An 18th-century engraving, showing Meleager presenting a boar's head to Atalanta.

forfeiting their lives if they lost. Eventually, Hippomenes won the race by dropping three golden apples during its course, each of which Atalanta stopped to recover, thus losing time. When Hippomenes forgot to thank Aphrodite for lending him the apples, both he and Atalanta were turned into leopards as a punishment. Some ancient Greeks believed that these animals did not mate.

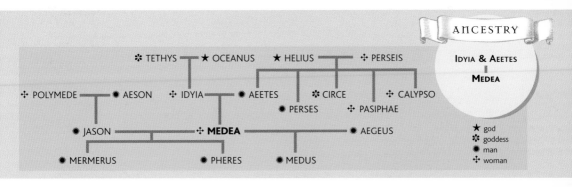

❋ TETHYS ━━ ★ OCEANUS   ★ HELIUS ━━ ✛ PERSEIS

✛ POLYMEDE ━━ ❋ AESON   ✛ IDYIA ━━ ❋ AEETES   ❋ CIRCE   ✛ CALYPSO

❋ PERSES   ✛ PASIPHAE

❋ JASON ━━ ✛ MEDEA ━━ ❋ AEGEUS

❋ MERMERUS   ❋ PHERES   ❋ MEDUS

IDYIA & AEETES

MEDEA

★ god
❋ goddess
❋ man
✛ woman

MEDEA

A powerful witch from Colchis in ancient Greece.

Medea fell in love with Jason, married him, and then helped him to steal the Golden Fleece which belonged to her father, Aeetes, king of Corinth. After leaving Colchis with Jason, Medea bore him two children, Mermerus and Pheres. When Jason sought to abandon her and marry Creusa, a Corinthian princess, Medea took revenge by poisoning Creusa's wedding gown so that it burned her to death. According to one version, Medea killed her own children.

IN ATHENS

Having taken her revenge on Jason and Creusa, Medea escaped to Athens in a magic chariot drawn by winged serpents, and was given shelter by Aegeus, father of Theseus. She soon married Aegeus and gave birth to a son, Medus. When Theseus claimed to be Aegeus' heir, Medea tried to persuade the king that Theseus, who had been away from Athens for many years, was

a spy. It was her intention that her own son should be Aegeus' heir. At a great feast at the Dolphin Temple in Athens, Medea's attempt to poison Theseus did not go according to plan. Amid much rejoicing, Aegeus embraced Theseus and acknowledged him as his son, while Medea fled with Medus to Italy, where she taught the art of snake-charming.

Another tradition says that Medea persuaded Aegeus to send Theseus to Crete in order to fight the deadly bull, the Minotaur. Only when the Minotaur was dead did Aegeus accept that Theseus was his rightful heir. Medea then returned to Colchis, where she succeeded in installing Medus as king.

IN LITERATURE

The major classical dramatists all wrote plays about this scheming sorceress. Euripides presented her sympathetically in *Medea* as a passionate feminist who was unable to control the ruinous forces within her, whereas Seneca's play of the same name stressed her savage witchcraft. In the Roman poet Ovid's *Metamorphoses*, she is a more romantic figure.

ROMAN FRESCO OF MEDEA AND JASON WITH THEIR SONS
A fresco painting from Pompeii shows Medea holding a sword while contemplating the murder of her sons.

THESEUS
AND THE
MINOTAUR

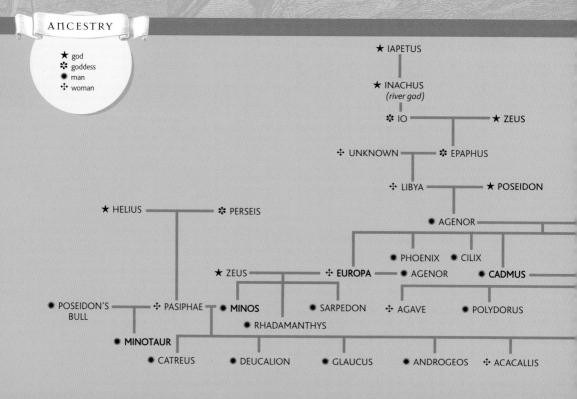

★ IAPETUS

★ INACHUS
(river god)

❀ IO — ★ ZEUS

✢ UNKNOWN — ❀ EPAPHUS

✢ LIBYA — ★ POSEIDON

★ HELIUS — ❀ PERSEIS

✹ AGENOR

✹ PHOENIX   ✹ CILIX

★ ZEUS — ✢ EUROPA — ✹ AGENOR   ✹ CADMUS

✹ POSEIDON'S BULL — ✢ PASIPHAE — ✹ MINOS   ✹ SARPEDON   ✢ AGAVE   ✹ POLYDORUS

✹ RHADAMANTHYS

✹ MINOTAUR   ✹ CATREUS   ✹ DEUCALION   ✹ GLAUCUS   ✹ ANDROGEOS   ✢ ACACALLIS

This cycle concerns the great Minoan myths of Crete. The beautiful Europa, future mother of King Minos, was carried off to the island by Zeus disguised as a white bull. The monstrous Minotaur, half-man, half-bull, lived there in the Labyrinth fashioned by the architect Daedalus. To stop the nine-yearly sacrifice of Athenian youths, Theseus, aided by Ariadne, navigated the Labyrinth, killed the Minotaur, and rescued its victims. Theseus was also engaged in a war against the female tribe of the Amazons, whose queen, Hippolyta, he married.

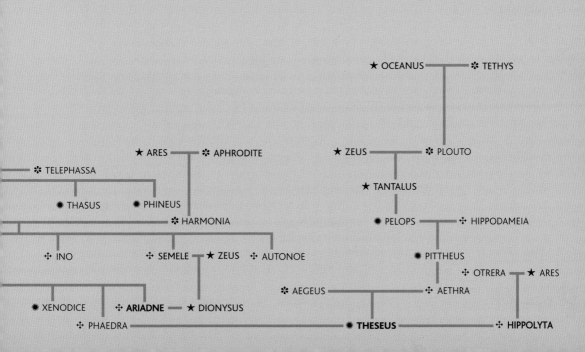

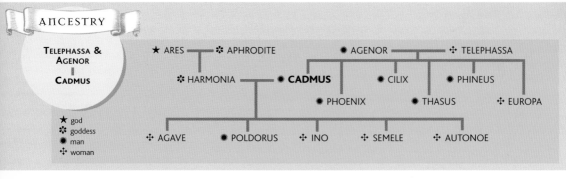

Family tree:

★ ARES ——— ❋ APHRODITE   ✢ AGENOR ——— ✣ TELEPHASSA

❋ HARMONIA ——— ✢ **CADMUS**   ✢ CILIX   ✢ PHINEUS

✢ PHOENIX   ✢ THASUS   ✣ EUROPA

✣ AGAVE   ✢ POLDORUS   ✣ INO   ✣ SEMELE   ✣ AUTONOE

C A D M U S

Hero of ancient Greece and founder of Thebes in Boeotia

When Europa was abducted by Zeus while he was disguised as a bull, her father, King Agenor of Tyre in Canaan, sent his five sons to rescue her. The eldest was Cadmus, and he became the natural leader. On consulting the Oracle at Delphi, however, Cadmus was advised to forget Europa, who was hidden in a cave on the island of Crete. Instead, he was told to find a cow marked with a moon-shaped sign on its flank. He was to follow the cow and found a city on the spot where the creature settled.

Cadmus followed the cow, which finally stopped in Boeotia, in central Greece. He determined that the animal should be sacrificed to Athena on the spot and he sent his followers to collect water from a nearby spring. But the spring was guarded by a dragon (some sources say a serpent) sacred to Ares, and it devoured most of the men alive.

Cadmus then slew the creature himself, crushing its head with a rock, and Athena appeared to advise him to remove the serpent's teeth and sow half of them in the ground. When he obeyed, armed men (known as the "Spartoi" or "Sown Men") appeared. Cadmus overcame them by throwing a stone among them so that each thought the other had hurled it and they brawled so ferociously that only five survived. These warriors became the ancestors of the Theban aristocracy.

Cadmus was obliged to serve Ares for eight years as a penance for killing the guardian monster. Once this period was over, however, Athena made Cadmus the king of Thebes and gave him splendid gifts. He built the Theban acropolis and married Harmonia, daughter of Aphrodite and Ares.

Thebes carried the guilt of its bloody foundation, because, of all the ancient Greek cities, it was the most troubled by legendary events. One of these occurred when Cadmus' grandson and successor, Pentheus, fell afoul of Dionysus by refusing to recognize his divinity. Pentheus tried to stop the worship of the god of wine and revelry, but was torn to pieces by Dionysus' frenzied devotees, the Maenads, who in their hysteria mistook Pentheus for a mountain lion.

In old age, Cadmus is said in some sources to have been turned into a snake. His importance as a cultural hero is reflected in his being credited with introducing to Europe an alphabet of sixteen letters.

CADMUS AND THE BOEOTIAN SERPENT
Sculpture of Cadmus, flanked by two youths, as he wrestles with a serpent. Some Thebans claimed descent from the teeth of this serpent, whose teeth Cadmus had planted in the soil. The statue is in the Gardens at the Palace of Versailles, France.

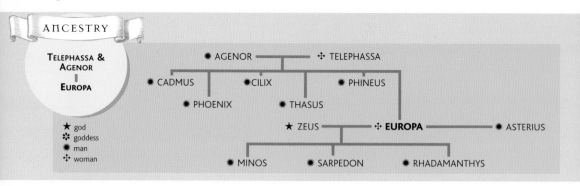

EUROPA

Important lover of Zeus and mother of King Minos of Crete.

Europa was the daughter of the Phoenician king, Agenor. Their home was in Tyre on the coast. One day, Europa was playing with her handmaidens by the sea when Zeus, king of the gods, appeared in the form of a majestic white bull. She found the animal so tame that she dared to climb on its back. Once astride, Europa found herself a prisoner, as Zeus galloped into the sea and swam to Crete, where he threw off his disguise and incarcerated her in a cave. There she gave birth to Minos, Sarpedon, and Rhadamanthys.

In gratitude, Zeus presented Europa with three gifts—a self-directed spear, an unbeatable hound, and a bronze man who breathed fire. He then left her and she eventually married Asterius, king of the Cretans. Since this was a childless marriage, the king was happy to adopt her semi-divine children and make them his heirs. One of them, Minos, succeeded him and became an infamous ruler.

Europa was an important figure on the island of Crete during the period of the great Minoan civilization that flourished there until the fifteenth century BC. The Minoans enjoyed bull-leaping and riding rituals, practices that are associated with her legend.

IN LITERATURE AND ART

The Roman poet Ovid described the amicable relationship of Europa and the bull, in which the friendly creature allowed the girl to garland his horns. The painter Titian depicted the same idea. Other artists who illustrated the story of Europa and the bull are Rubens, Veronese, and Rembrandt, and, in the modern period, Moreau and Matisse.

THE RAPE OF EUROPA
François Boucher's 1747 oil painting stylizes the story of the Phoenician princess raped by Zeus, who was then disguised in the form of a white bull.

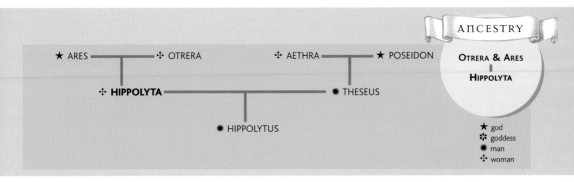

★ ARES ——— ✣ OTRERA   ✣ AETHRA ——— ★ POSEIDON

✣ HIPPOLYTA ————————————— ✳ THESEUS

✳ HIPPOLYTUS

★ god
✣ goddess
✳ man
✣ woman

HIPPOLYTA

Queen of the Amazons, a nation of warrior women in Greek mythology.

The Amazons were a curious nation of women, supposedly children of Ares who inhabited the Amazonian mountains of Phrygia (in modern Turkey). Their great skill was in warfare, and their most famous queen was Hippolyta.

Of their many customs, the most peculiar was the removal of their right breast to facilitate the launching of javelins and arrows. The left breast was kept intact for suckling babies. These warrior women rode into battle on horseback and were allowed to mate only after killing a man. As males were forbidden among their ranks, members of another tribe or race had to be sought for sexual intercourse. Any male offspring were killed or given to their fathers.

THE GOLDEN GIRDLE
For his ninth labor, Heracles had to recover the golden girdle of Ares, which Hippolyta possessed as a symbol of her supremacy among the Amazons. Heracles sailed with a company of volunteers, including Theseus, Peleus, and Telamon, to the River Thermodon in Phrygia. On arrival, Heracles was met by Hippolyta, who promised to give him the girdle. Then the goddess

Hera disguised herself as an Amazon and started a rumor that Heracles was going to abduct their queen. Taking up arms, the warrior-women charged out to the harbor. Seeing their hostility, Heracles suspected a plot and attacked them, killing Hippolyta and robbing her of the girdle. Heracles and his companions fought off the other Amazons until those remaining were forced to flee. Some sources say Hippolyta did not die, but was abducted by Theseus and became his wife in Athens, where she bore him a son, Hippolytus.

THESEUS
One tradition says that as a reward for his part in the campaign, Theseus was given Antiope as a wife. This was not such a dreadful outcome for the Amazon, because she was said to be in love with him already and had proved as much by betraying the city of Themiscyra to him. Another version of the story says that Theseus abducted Antiope, and in revenge the Amazons invaded his city of Athens. A long, hard-fought war ended with the decimation of the Amazons.

FEMALE WARRIORS
A Greek soldier pursues a wounded Amazon in battle.

MINOS

Legendary king of Crete, son of Zeus and Europa.

The three sons of Europa by Zeus, who carried her off to Crete disguised as a bull, were adopted by the Cretan king, Asterius. When it was time for a successor to the throne to be appointed, a dispute broke out between the brothers over who would be the next king. This was decided when Minos prayed to the sea god Poseidon for a divine sign, and the god sent him a magnificent bull from the sea. However, because Minos neglected to sacrifice the bull, Poseidon cursed him, and Minos' wife Pasiphae fell madly in love with the creature.

With the aid of the craftsman Daedalus, who was living in exile at Knossos on Crete, Pasiphae was able to satisfy her lust by adopting a coital position inside a decoy cow Daedalus built especially for the purpose. The result of this strange union was the Minotaur, a monster with a bull's head and a man's body. Anxious to avoid disgrace falling on his wife, Minos consulted an oracle. He was told to build a retreat at Knossos with a maze in which he, his wife, and the Minotaur could dwell in secrecy. Minos obediently commissioned Daedalus to build a maze known as the Labyrinth.

According to Athenian tradition, Minos insisted that each year seven boys and seven girls should be sent from Athens to the Labyrinth as food for the Minotaur. One year, the hero Theseus was selected for sacrifice, but he succeeded in killing the beast and, furthermore, ran off with Minos' daughter Ariadne, who had helped him to escape.

Daedalus, who was also involved in the plot, fled to Sicily with his son, Icarus, who died when the wax on his wings melted and he plunged to earth during the escape. Minos pursued Daedalus, but the inventor avenged his son's death by arranging for boiling oil to kill the king when he took a bath at Kamikos.

In history, the real King Minos possessed a powerful navy that made him a fearsome enemy. The unfavorable stories about him may have arisen from the wars he waged against rival kings on the Greek mainland. He was, though, renowned for being a wise governor of his island people.

MINOS, KING OF CRETE
An engraving by the French printmaker Gustave Dore of King Minos of Crete, depicting a scene from Dante's Inferno.

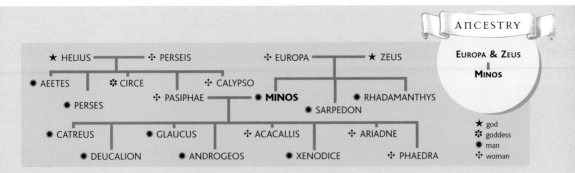

ANCESTRY

EUROPA & ZEUS
|
MINOS

★ HELIUS ✛ PERSEIS ✛ EUROPA ★ ZEUS

✹ AEETES ❀ CIRCE ✛ CALYPSO

✹ PERSES ✛ PASIPHAE ✹ MINOS ✹ RHADAMANTHYS

✹ SARPEDON

✹ CATREUS ✹ GLAUCUS ✛ ACACALLIS ✛ ARIADNE

✹ DEUCALION ✹ ANDROGEOS ✛ XENODICE ✛ PHAEDRA

★ god
❀ goddess
✹ man
✛ woman

DAEDALUS

Legendary Greek architect and inventor who created the Minotaur's Labyrinth in Crete, and father of Icarus.

Daedalus, whose name in Greek means "ingenious," was a gifted craftsman. His statues were so lifelike that they were chained up in case they sprang to life and ran away. As well as works of art, his skills included designing splendid palaces and constructing impressive machines.

Despite his renowned talents, competition from his nephew and pupil Talus in Athens unsettled Daedalus. When the young apprentice invented the saw by copying the jaw of a serpent, Daedalus feared he might surpass his own skills and, in a fit of jealousy, hurled the boy down from the Acropolis. In a trial for the murder at the Areopagus court, Daedalus was found guilty and exiled to Crete.

The quarrel between Daedalus and Talus may have its origins in some ancient rivalry over the invention of metal tools. Like other ancient peoples, the Greeks were conscious that they were dependent on such advances in technology. Certainly, the services of a talented man like Daedalus were appreciated by ancient rulers.

At the command of Minos, king of Crete, Daedalus designed the king's palace and built the maze known as the Labyrinth as a home for the monstrous Minotaur, a creature with a bull's head and a man's body. He also devised an ingenious decoy cow to entice the magnificent bull that Poseidon sent to Minos. The model was made of wood and mounted on wheels, then covered in hide to convince the bull that it was authentic. Daedalus then helped Pasiphae, Minos' wife who had been cursed with an insatiable lust for the bull, to climb inside and wait to be satisfied.

ICARUS

Minos was angered by Daedalus. Whether it was due to his piece of cunning handiwork or because Daedalus later revealed the layout of the Labyrinth to Theseus, Minos was so enraged that he threw him and his son Icarus (born of a slave of Minos) into prison, which some say was the Labyrinth. Even here the inventor was able to devise an ingenious method of escape. With wings made from feathers embedded in wax, the prisoners were able to fly away, but Daedalus cautioned Icarus to proceed carefully to avoid the sun's heat on the wax and the weight of sea spray on the feathers. But Icarus was so exhilarated by the new experience of flight that he flew too near the sun. The wax melted, his wings fell apart, and the hapless boy plunged into the sea.

EXILE IN SICILY

After burying his son, Daedalus went to live in Sicily, still in hiding from Minos. He was popular with the islanders, making beautiful toys for their children and building homes. Before long, Minos visited the island and discovered the exile. The local ruler, King Cocalus, was overawed by Minos' powerful fleet and promised to surrender the architect, but first he insisted that his guest should follow their custom of indulging in a luxurious bath attended by princesses. Inventive as ever, Daedalus laid a pipe through the roof of the bathroom, down which the girls poured boiling oil, burning the unsuspecting Minos to death.

THE FALL OF ICARUS
Ceiling fresco of the rotunda of Apollo, 1796.

ALCIPPE &
EUPALAMUS
|
DAEDALUS

★ EUPALAMUS ── ✣ ALCIPPE

(UNKNOWN) ── ✣ POLYCASTE　　DAEDALUS ── ✣ NAUCRATE
Slave of Minos

✱ TALUS　　✱ ICARUS　　✱ IAPYX

★ god
✺ goddess
✱ man
✣ woman

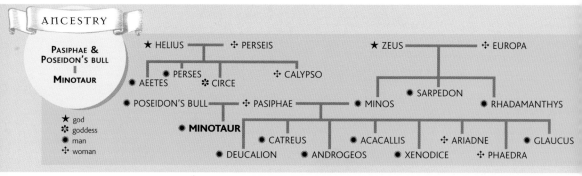

PASIPHAE &
POSEIDON'S BULL
|
MINOTAUR

★ HELIUS ━━━━━ ✣ PERSEIS   ★ ZEUS ━━━━━ ✣ EUROPA

✣ PERSES   ✣ CALYPSO
❋ AEETES ✢ CIRCE   ❋ SARPEDON

❋ POSEIDON'S BULL ━━ ✣ PASIPHAE ━━━ ❋ MINOS   ❋ RHADAMANTHYS

★ god
✢ goddess   ❋ MINOTAUR
❋ man
✣ woman   ❋ CATREUS   ❋ ACACALLIS   ✣ ARIADNE   ❋ GLAUCUS
          ❋ DEUCALION   ❋ ANDROGEOS   ❋ XENODICE   ✣ PHAEDRA

MINOTAUR

In Greek mythology, a monster with a bull's head and a man's body.

The Greek meaning of Minotaur is "Minos' bull," which refers to the creature's parentage. It was the strange offspring of Pasiphae, wife of King Minos of Crete, and a handsome bull sent from the sea by Poseidon with which she fell in love. The craftsman Daedalus made a decoy cow so that Pasiphae could satisfy her lustful desire, imposed on her by Poseidon as a punishment for Minos' failure to sacrifice the bull to the god.

THE LABYRINTH

The Minotaur was confined to the maze known as the Labyrinth. Anyone entering it found it impossible to escape because of its many winding passages. Each year King Minos ordered the Athenians to send seven boys and seven girls to his palace at Knossos as food for the monster.

One year, Theseus volunteered to go to the Labyrinth as a sacrificial victim. When he arrived on the island of Crete, Minos' daughter Ariadne fell in love with the dashing hero and offered to help him in his task if he would take her to Athens with him afterward and marry her. He happily agreed and the girl gave him a ball of thread which he attached to the doorpost at the entrance to the maze and let it unravel as he progressed to the heart of the Labyrinth. Finding the monster asleep, Theseus crept up on it and beat it to death with his bare fists (some say with a sword given him by Ariadne), and made his way back to the entrance by following the thread.

IN ART

The Minotaur has been a fascinating inspiration for painters and sculptors. Picasso saw the monster as symbolizing humanity's animal nature liberated from the intellect. For the French painter Gide, the Minotaur was an image of erotic fascination, while for American sculptor Michael Ayrton the Labyrinth represents doubt and confusion, as well as people's desire to be rid of their animal form. In New York, Ayrton has built an immense stone maze containing sculptures of the Minotaur, Daedalus, and Icarus.

THESEUS AND THE MINOTAUR
Mosaic in the House of the Labyrinth at Pompeii.

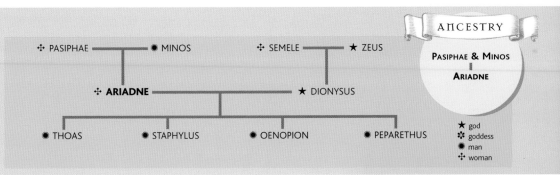

PASIPHAE — MINOS   SEMELE — ZEUS

ARIADNE — DIONYSUS

THOAS   STAPHYLUS   OENOPION   PEPARETHUS

★ god
✣ goddess
✱ man
✣ woman

ARIADNE

Daughter of King Minos who helped Theseus escape from Crete.

While Theseus sojourned on Crete, offering himself as a sacrificial victim to the Minotaur, Aphrodite was on his mind. Not only did he sleep with two Athenian maidens, he instantly attracted Minos' daughter Ariadne, who fell madly in love with him. When she offered to help Theseus in his task of slaying her half-brother monster if he would take her away with him and marry her, he readily agreed. With advice from the craftsman Daedalus, who had designed the Labyrinth in which the monster lived, she successfully guided her lover through it by means of a ball of thread. When eventually he emerged, spattered with blood but triumphant, Ariadne passionately embraced the intrepid hero.

The two lovers stole away secretly in the night, together with the boys and girls saved from the yearly tribute. Days later, they arrived at the island of Naxos but there, strangely, Theseus appeared to have a change of heart and left Ariadne asleep on the shore while he sailed away. Various explanations have been suggested for Theseus' betrayal. One was that while ashore he reflected on the scandal Ariadne's arrival in Athens would cause, as she was the half-sister of the Minotaur, the monster with a bull's head and a man's body. Another tradition says the god Dionysus appeared to Theseus in a dream and demanded Ariadne for himself, and under this spell the hero took off in fright.

Whatever the reason, Ariadne was inconsolable when she discovered that her lover had gone away. Remembering the risks she had run and how she had deserted her parents, the spurned king's daughter's sorrow soon turned to bitter resentment. Her cry to the gods for vengeance was answered by Zeus, who sent Dionysus to her rescue. The lustful god of wine took her to be his wife and the couple sped off to the island of Lemnos where they had four children: Thoas, Staphylus, Oenopion,

DIONYSUS AND ARIADNE
An early 18th-century painting by Sebastiano Ricci telling the story of how Dionysus (Bacchus) found Ariadne desolate on Naxos and fell in love with her.

and Peparethus. Ariadne was granted a crown of seven stars which became a constellation on her death.

Ariadne's betrayal by Theseus was a common theme among later poets and artists, especially the idea that life could be found through death as a result of divine intervention.

THESEUS

*Legendary Greek hero and champion
of the Athenians.*

The Athenians credited
Theseus with numerous
exploits, including the
foundation of their own city-
state. Among the many triumphs
of the hero was his encounter
with Sinis, the pine-bender.
Controlling the narrow Isthmus
of Corinth, Sinis would force
travelers to bend pine trees to the
ground and hold them down
until they became too weak.
When they let go, they would be
hurled into the air to their death.
Theseus was strong enough to
overcome Sinis and killed him
by his own method.

MINOTAUR SLAYER

There were many other occasions
when this great public servant
came to the aid of travelers who
fell afoul of local menaces. Above
all, however, Theseus was
celebrated for slaying the
Minotaur, the monstrous bull-
headed man that lived in the
Labyrinth of the Cretan King
Minos. In a peace treaty with
Minos, the Athenians agreed to
send a yearly tribute of seven
boys and seven girls to Crete as
food for the Minotaur. Theseus
took pity on their parents and
volunteered to be included in the
list of the children who were due
to be sent to the dreaded place,
an offer that deeply upset his

father Aegeus. Theseus calmed
his father's fears by telling him to
look for the color of his ship's sail
on its return from Crete. If it had
been changed from black to
white, he would know that his
son was still alive.

Having slain the monster,
Theseus escaped with Minos'
daughter, Ariadne, whom he had
promised to marry. For some
unknown reason, however, he
reneged on his promise and

deserted her on Naxos. So
preoccupied was he with this
matter that he forgot to change
his ship's sail. When, from a
distance, Aegeus saw the black
sail, he assumed that his son was
dead and flung himself off a cliff
in despair.

KING OF ATHENS

Theseus became king and unified
the Athenians into a single state.
Despite his position, Theseus

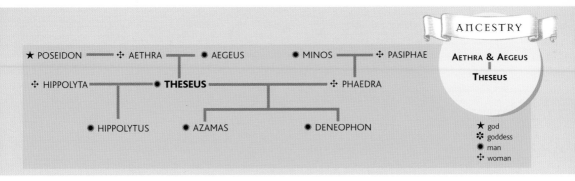

★ POSEIDON ── ✛ AETHRA ── ✲ AEGEUS   ✲ MINOS ── ✛ PASIPHAE

✛ HIPPOLYTA ── **THESEUS** ── ✛ PHAEDRA

✲ HIPPOLYTUS   ✲ AZAMAS   ✲ DENEOPHON

★ god
✲ goddess
✲ man
✛ woman

continued his adventures, which included accompanying Heracles on his expedition to fight the fierce female warrior Amazons, whose queen, Hippolyta, Theseus married. Although he had a son, Hippolytus, by her, the Athenian later took Phaedra, daughter of Minos, as his wife, probably as a peace initiative. Eventually, various tragedies befell Theseus before he retired to the palace of Lycomedes, king of Scyros, who threw the hero into an abyss, fearing he would be usurped.

FEUD

A friend of Theseus was Perithoos the Lapith. One day he married Hippodameia, and to their wedding were invited her relatives the Centaurs. Unused to alcohol, they became drunk on the wine and riotous, abusing the bride and guests. Perithoos and Theseus sprang to Hippodameia's rescue and a fight ensued lasting till nightfall. Thereafter a long feud continued between the Centaurs and their Lapith neighbors.

DESERTING ARIADNE
In his haste to leave Ariadne on the island of Naxos, Theseus set sail with his black sail hoisted, a sign that led his father to think he had been killed by the Minotaur.

PERSEUS

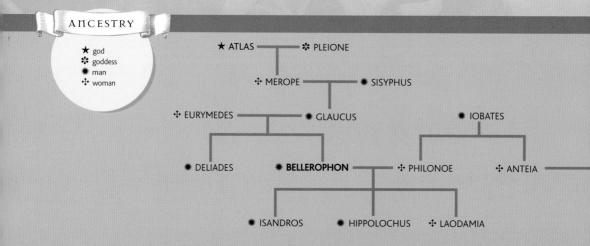

★ ATLAS — ❋ PLEIONE

✣ MEROPE — ✹ SISYPHUS

✣ EURYMEDES — ✹ GLAUCUS   ✹ IOBATES

✹ DELIADES   ✹ **BELLEROPHON**   ✣ PHILONOE   ✣ ANTEIA

✹ ISANDROS   ✹ HIPPOLOCHUS   ✣ LAODAMIA

W orshiped as divine in Athens, Perseus was one of the great heroes of ancient Greece. The mission of Perseus, son of Zeus and Danäe, was to kill the fearful Medusa, a glimpse of whom would turn her victim to stone. Aided by the gods, the hero succeeded in his task. Meanwhile, Medusa's spilt blood created the horse Pegasus which, later, Bellerophon tried to ride to heaven, incurring the wrath of the gods. Perseus also rescued Andromeda from the rocks and with her founded the family of the Perseids (people of Persia), from whom Heracles was descended.

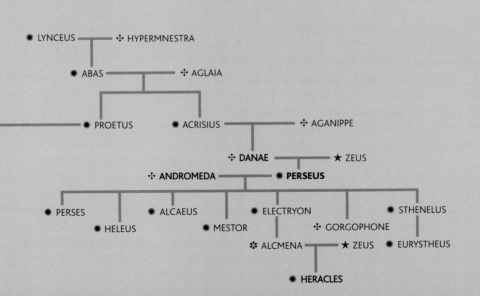

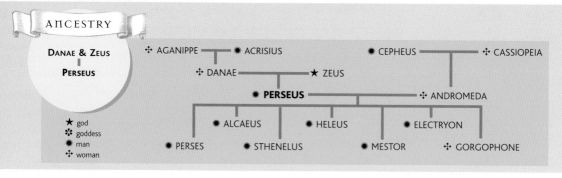

DANAE & ZEUS

PERSEUS

✤ AGANIPPE ——— ✱ ACRISIUS   ✱ CEPHEUS ——————— ✤ CASSIOPEIA

✤ DANAE —————— ★ ZEUS

✱ **PERSEUS** ——————————— ✤ ANDROMEDA

✱ ALCAEUS   ✱ HELEUS   ✱ ELECTRYON

✱ PERSES   ✱ STHENELUS   ✱ MESTOR   ✤ GORGOPHONE

★ god
✱ goddess
✱ man
✤ woman

PERSEUS

Greek hero who killed Medusa, chief of the dreaded Gorgons.

A prophecy foretold that Danae, an Argive princess, would bear a son who would kill his grandfather, the king. To prevent this from happening, the king locked Danae in a bronze tower. However, Zeus, disguised as a golden shower, poured through the roof into her lap. The result of their union was the birth of Perseus. Afterward, Zeus spirited away both mother and child.

Perseus was brought up either in obscurity among fishermen or by a local ruler, Polydectes.

Perseus soon showed his worth by defending Danae from the advances of Polydectes, who wished to marry her against her will. To rid himself of the hero, the ruler ordered Perseus to fetch him the head of Medusa, one of the three frightening Gorgon sisters; her features were so terrible that anyone who looked upon her was turned to stone.

Medusa had serpents instead of hair, golden wings, claws of bronze, and glaring eyes. Because she had desecrated the temple of Athena, the goddess gave Perseus a magic shield for his protection. And, as tokens of her admiration for the hero's courage, Hermes, the winged god, presented him with a cap of invisibility, a sharp sword, and winged shoes.

Having discovered their whereabouts, Perseus found the three Gorgons asleep. Nevertheless, because he would have been killed merely by glancing at Medusa directly, he approached the monster by looking at her reflection in his shield. Then he cut off her head and made his escape, helped by the cap of invisibility.

A different legend relates how Athena decapitated Medusa and buried her head under the marketplace at Athens. Whatever the role of the hero in this adventure, Perseus went on to slay other monsters which harried mankind. He also accidentally killed his grandfather with a discus, thus fulfilling the prophecy.

MEDUSA SLAIN
Perseus holding up the head of the Gorgon Medusa in order to turn his assailant Phineus into stone.

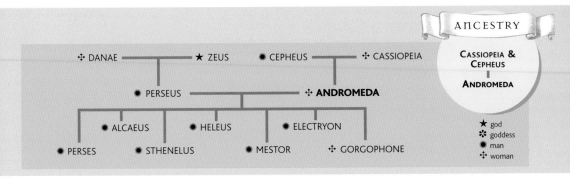

DANAE ———— ★ ZEUS ✹ CEPHEUS ———— ✢ CASSIOPEIA

✹ PERSEUS ———————— ✢ ANDROMEDA

✹ ALCAEUS ✹ HELEUS ✹ ELECTRYON

✹ PERSES ✹ STHENELUS ✹ MESTOR ✢ GORGOPHONE

★ god
✹ goddess
✹ man
✢ woman

ANDROMEDA

Wife of the Greek hero Perseus.

Trouble began for this daughter of Casseopeia and Cepheus, the Ethiopian king of Joppa in Philistia (coast of Palestine), when her mother boasted of her own and Andromeda's great beauty. Her claim that they outshone the Nereids so incensed these sea nymphs that they complained to their protector Poseidon. As a punishment, the god sent a tidal flood over Philistia, as well as a sea monster to ravage the inhabitants.

When King Cepheus consulted the oracle of Ammon for advice, he was told his only hope was to sacrifice his daughter to the monster. Horrified though he was at such a prospect, his subjects forced his hand and he had Andromeda chained, naked except for some jewels, to a rock on the cliff, ready to be devoured.

Now it so happened that Perseus had just cut off Medusa's head and was flying over the area when he spotted Andromeda. Instantly he fell in love with her and, seeing her distraught parents nearby, came to speak to them. They made an agreement that if Perseus saved the girl he would be allowed to marry her

The winged hero took to the air again and, grasping his sickle, dived down to the sea where the monster lurked in readiness for his prey. Deceived by the shadow of Perseus on the sea, the monster failed to evade the swinging blow of the hero's sickle and was decapitated.

A jubilant Perseus rescued Andromeda and returned to Cepheus and Cassiopeia. Delighted though the parents were to see their daughter safe and unharmed, they broke their promise to Perseus, claiming they were unable to agree to his terms and that a prior betrothal to Agenor must be honored. When Perseus insisted on his prize, Cassiopeia declared that Perseus must die. An ensuing fight resulted in the outnumbered hero defeating all his opponents using his special weapon, the head of Medusa, which he kept tucked under his arm. Whoever he turned the Gorgon's face toward was turned to stone.

Thus victorious, Perseus finally won Andromeda, who had herself wished to marry Perseus, whom she loved. Together they had many children, including Perses, from whom it is said were descended the kings of Persia and the hero Heracles.

PERSEUS AND ANDROMEDA
Perseus, riding the winged Pegasus, rescues Andromeda from her fate as a sacrifice to Poseidon's monster.

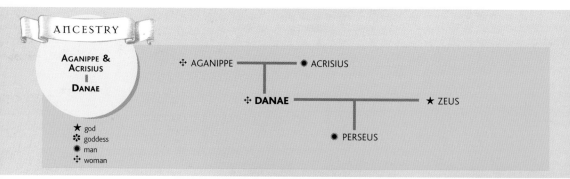

ANCESTRY

AGANIPPE &
ACRISIUS
|
DANAE

✦ AGANIPPE ──────── ✹ ACRISIUS

✦ DANAE ──────────── ★ ZEUS

✹ PERSEUS

★ god
✹ goddess
✹ man
✦ woman

DANAE

*Mother of the hero Perseus
by Zeus.*

anae is at the center of a legend in which an oracle warns her father Acrisius, king of Argos, that his daughter would have a son who would murder him. Acrisius was married to Aganippe, had no sons, and just one daughter. The king took no chances and imprisoned Danae in a bronze chamber guarded by vicious dogs. However, Zeus came to her rescue, and, taking the form of a golden shower, he poured through the roof into her lap. Their union produced a son named Perseus.

When Acrisius was told what had happened, he refused to believe that Zeus was involved and immediately suspected his twin brother, Proetus, with whom he was in dispute over the inheritance of their father's land of Argos. Traditions differ about the next events. Some say that Zeus spirited away both mother and child; others relate that Acrisius put both mother and child into a chest and threw it into the sea. Eventually, the chest was washed ashore, and was discovered by a fisherman named Dictys who, on breaking open the box, discovered Danae and the infant still alive. He took them to his brother, King Polydectes, who fell in love with Danae and brought up Perseus as his own son.

However, tradition has it that a conflict arose between Perseus and Polydectes, who was secretly trying to persuade Danae to marry him. The king pretended to be interested in Hippodameia, daughter of King Pelops, but Perseus was determined to call his bluff and promised the suitor that if he vowed not to marry Danae, he would endeavor to

SHOWER OF GOLD *Zeus visited the captive Danae in the form of a shower of gold. From their union, the hero Perseus was born.*

win any prize Polydectes should care to name, even the head of a Gorgon. With little hesitation, Polydectes ordered him to fetch the head of Medusa. When Perseus had accomplished this feat with the help of Athena, he returned to take his revenge on Polydectes.

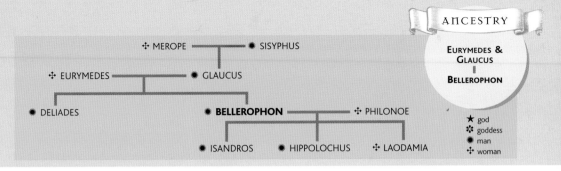

✧ MEROPE ——— ✹ SISYPHUS

✧ EURYMEDES ——— ✹ GLAUCUS

✹ DELIADES ✹ **BELLEROPHON** ——— ✧ PHILONOE

✹ ISANDROS ✹ HIPPOLOCHUS ✧ LAODAMIA

★ god
✹ goddess
✹ man
✧ woman

BELLEROPHON

*Son of Glaucus, king of Corinth, and rider of the winged
horse Pegasus.*

This grandson of Sisyphus—the man destined to spend his days pushing a boulder up a mountain—was a similar hero to Heracles, who had also been assigned a series of tasks to complete for his survival. He was originally named Hipponous, but was forced to change his name after accidentally killing his brother Deliades and then a nobleman named Bellerus (Bellerophon in Greek means "Bellerus slayer"). He fled to the court of Proetus, king of Tiryns, where Queen Anteia instantly fell in love with him. Bellerophon rejected her advances and she accused him of seducing her in a

story her husband believed. Unwilling to do harm to a royal guest, Proetus sent him with a letter of explanation to his father-in-law, Iobates, king of Lycia, who dealt Bellerophon a series of challenges he was not expected to survive.

With the aid of his winged horse Pegasus, he successfully met the first challenge of destroying the Chimaera, a strange fire-breathing creature consisting of a lion's head, a serpent's tail, and a goat in the middle, born of the monster Typhon. After passing further tests, including defeating the Amazons by riding Pegasus high over their heads out of bowshot

and bombarding them with rocks, Bellerophon was finally reprieved. On discovering the truth behind Anteia's tale, Iobates begged Bellerophon's forgiveness and rewarded him with the hand of his other daughter, Philonoe, in marriage.

For attempting to ride Pegasus to the top of Mount Olympus, Bellerophon was flung down to earth by Zeus, and spent the rest of his days wandering alone, blind and crippled. Unlike Heracles, however, Bellerophon failed to attain immortality.

BELLEROPHON AND PEGASUS
*Bellerophon is shown here riding
Pegasus, armed and ready to fight
the Chimaera.*

PEGASUS: WINGED HORSE OF BELLEROPHON

When Perseus slew the Gorgon Medusa, the winged horse Pegasus grew from the blood flowing from her dead body. This creature originated from Poseidon's seduction of Medusa when she was still beautiful and not the hideous monster she was turned into by Athena. Pegasus was believed to be the moon-horse who was employed in making rain. To achieve sacred kingship, candidates were given the task of capturing and taming a wild horse. Bellerophon tamed Pegasus with a special bridle made by Athena after he had caught the horse drinking at a spring.

HERACLES/HERCULES

Great hero of the Greeks, known to the Romans as Hercules,
who famously performed twelve labors for King Eurystheus.

Heracles was the son of Zeus and Alcmena, Queen of Tiryns. Zeus' jealous wife, Hera, delayed the birth in order to prevent Heracles from becoming king of Tiryns. By retarding his birth, another child was born who inherited the crown, and Heracles became a slave instead.

Heracles' semi-divine nature soon became evident, however. When Hera sent two snakes to kill him in his cot, the baby Heracles seized one in each hand and strangled them. His prowess with the spear and arrow, as well as in wrestling, became renowned. But Hera was not to be thwarted, and she struck him with a fit of madness, which led him to tragically kill his own wife, Megara, and sons.

Unable to find peace of mind, Heracles consulted the Oracle at Delphi. There he was told to go to Tiryns and obey the orders of its king, Eurystheus, who then set the hero a number of tasks or "labors."

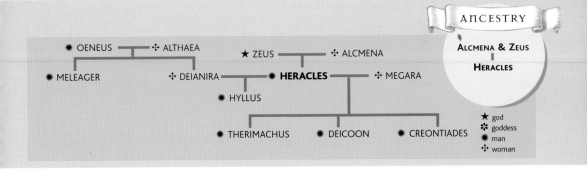

ANCESTRY
ALCMENA & ZEUS
|
HERACLES

OENEUS ⚛ ALTHAEA   ★ ZEUS ⚛ ALCMENA

MELEAGER   ⚛ DEIANIRA ⚛ HERACLES ⚛ MEGARA

HYLLUS

THERIMACHUS   DEICOON   CREONTIADES

★ god
⚛ goddess
⚛ man
⚛ woman

THE TWELVE LABORS

Heracles' first task was to destroy the Nemean lion, a fierce beast that was terrorizing the countryside around Tiryns. When Heracles found that the lion could not be harmed even by magic arrows provided by Apollo, he resorted to using his own bare hands. After a great struggle, Heracles throttled the beast and took the skin for a trophy. Zeus then turned the dead Nemean lion into the constellation Leo.

The second labor was to kill the Hydra, a nine-headed serpent that was sacred to Hera. Heracles found that no sooner had he cut off one head than two more sprang up. He called for help from his nephew Iolaus who, after each decapitation, burned the serpentine stump with a torch. When Heracles was at last victorious, Eurystheus did not acknowledge the success of the labor because the hero had enlisted help.

The third labor was to capture the Cerynitian hind, a golden-horned creature that was sacred

to Artemis. Heracles captured it in Arcadia and released it unharmed at Tiryns.

Still in Arcadia, Heracles' fourth labor involved capturing the Erymanthian boar by shouting outside its lair and trapping it in a snowdrift when it rushed out.

Hercules' fifth labor was to clean the stables belonging to King Augeas, son of Helius. His vast herds had deposited dung so deep that Heracles could clear it away only by diverting a river. Again, the success of this labor was discounted because the hero received payment.

The sixth labor was to kill the vicious Stymphalian birds that terrorized the area with their steel-tipped wings. Heracles shot many with arrows; the rest he drove off using a bronze rattle made by Hephaestus.

The next labor took Heracles to Crete. There he captured the sea-born bull that Minos had failed to sacrifice to Poseidon, and brought it back to Tiryns.

For the eighth labor Heracles tamed the wild, man-eating horses of Diomedes of Thrace. En route, he saved a Thessalian queen by wrestling Thanatos (Death) to the ground.

The ninth labor was more difficult and involved acquiring

the golden girdle of Hippolyta, queen of the Amazons.

The next labor took Heracles to Spain. As he passed the Straits of Gibraltar on his way, the hero set up the twin Pillars of Hercules. Then he had to raid a cattle-farmer, King Geryon, who had three heads, six hands, and three bodies joined at the waist, and then drive the oxen overland to Tiryns, where Eurystheus sacrificed them to Hera.

The final two labors had to be performed because Eurystheus did not accept the success of the second and fifth tasks. The eleventh labor involved fetching the golden apples of the Hesperides (see *Atlas*).

The twelfth and last labor was to bring the three-headed dog Cerberus from the Underworld. By succeeding in this task, Heracles overcame Hades, King of the Dead.

Heracles' second wife, Deianira, was afraid that Heracles would desert her. The crafty centaur Nessus deceived her into believing that the power of his blood would enable her to retain Heracles' favor. Not realizing that it was toxic, Deianira sprinkled it on her husband's tunic. Heracles was fatally poisoned and thus the great hero's mortal life came to an end.

THE APOTHEOSIS OF HERCULES
An 18th-century ceiling fresco showing the ascent of Heracles to Mount Olympus as an immortal.

OEDIPUS

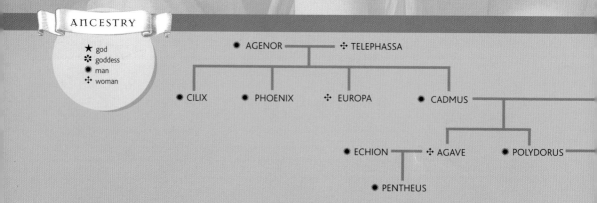

✳ AGENOR ——— ✤ TELEPHASSA

✳ CILIX   ✳ PHOENIX   ✤ EUROPA   ✳ CADMUS

✳ ECHION   ✤ AGAVE   ✳ POLYDORUS

✳ PENTHEUS

One of the best known tragedies of Greek mythology revolves around the character of Oedipus of the House of Thebes. This son of Laius unwittingly married his own mother, Jocasta, after having killed his father in an argument. This fulfilled the oracle of Delphi, the horror of which had dogged Oedipus until it came true. When Oedipus solved the riddle of the Sphinx who was ravaging Thebes, he was offered kingship of the city-state. But the revelation by Tiresias, the seer of Oedipus' patricide, had further tragic repercussions when Jocasta committed suicide, and Oedipus mutilated himself in disgust and was banished from his homeland.

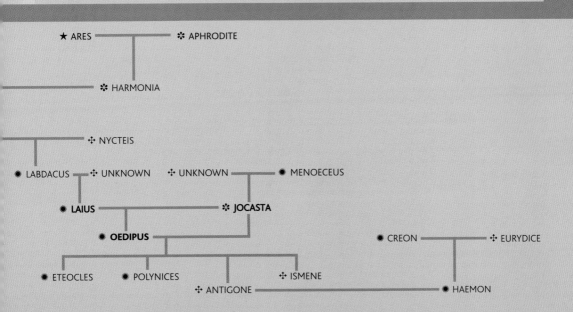

OEDIPUS

Infamous Greek prince who killed his father and married his mother; the only man to solve the riddle of the Sphinx.

Oedipus' father, Laius, king of Thebes, was warned that he would be murdered by any son born by his wife Jocasta. So when she gave birth to a boy, the king ordered that the newborn baby should be taken to a mountain and left to die. First, Laius pierced the infant's feet with a nail and bound them together. But the Fates had decreed that the child should live, and a shepherd found him, and named him Oedipus (meaning in Greek "swollen foot"). The baby was then given to a peasant who passed him to Polybus, king of Corinth, who was childless and happy to adopt the boy.

When Oedipus grew up, he was taunted about his uncertain parentage. On inquiry, the Oracle at Delphi told him that he would kill his father and marry his mother. Horrified, Oedipus immediately fled the court at Corinth, vowing never again to see Polybus and his wife, whom he believed were his parents.

MURDER AND INCEST

On the road to Thebes, Oedipus encountered a stranger whom he killed in a quarrel over the right of way. The victim turned out to be Laius, his true father.

Unknown to Oedipus, the first part of the prophecy had been fulfilled.

Oedipus then risked his life by attempting to solve a riddle posed by the Sphinx, a dangerous monster and daughter of Typhon that was plaguing Thebes. Her form was easily recognized, having a woman's head, a lion's body, a serpent's tail, and an eagle's wings. By successfully answering the riddle, Oedipus rid the Thebans of the Sphinx and was rewarded with the vacant throne and the hand in marriage of his widowed mother, Jocasta, whom, of course, he had never known. The union produced two sons, Eteocles and Polynices, and two daughters, Antigone and Ismene.

When eventually Oedipus became aware that he had committed both patricide and incest, he was driven to blind himself in remorse and, receiving no help from his sons, was expelled from the city and turned into an exile. The tragedy unfolded further when Jocasta hanged herself after she discovered that she had married her own son. Oedipus lived out his days near Athens, where he was given sanctuary by Theseus and then mysteriously disappeared in a sacred grove.

IN LITERATURE AND PSYCHOANALYSIS

Sophocles' play *Oedipus at Colonnus* influenced such modern writers as Shelley and W.B. Yeats, and T.S. Eliot in his play *The Elder Statesman*. There are many variations on the theme of the Oedipus story. One of the most individualistic has come from the French moralist André Gide, who saw Oedipus as a symbol of mankind's desire to act independently of conventional tradition (as represented by Tiresias and Creon). According to Gide, it was only when blind that Oedipus was able to answer riddles for mankind.

The psychoanalyst Sigmund Freud used the figure of Oedipus to illuminate one of his theories, the Oedipus complex.

OEDIPUS AND THE SPHINX
Oedipus answering the riddle of the Sphinx.

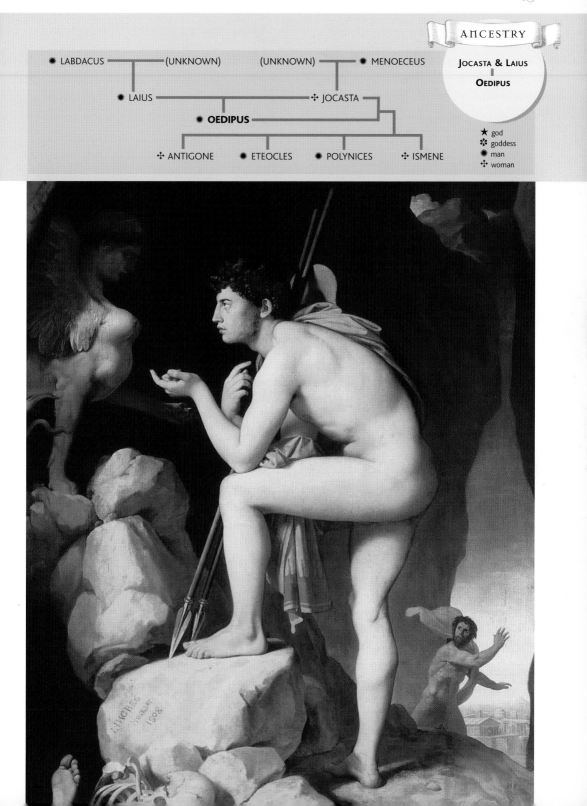

★ LABDACUS ——————— (UNKNOWN)   (UNKNOWN) ——————— ★ MENOECEUS

★ LAIUS ————————————————— ✣ JOCASTA

★ **OEDIPUS**

✣ ANTIGONE   ★ ETEOCLES   ★ POLYNICES   ✣ ISMENE

★ god
✳ goddess
✷ man
✣ woman

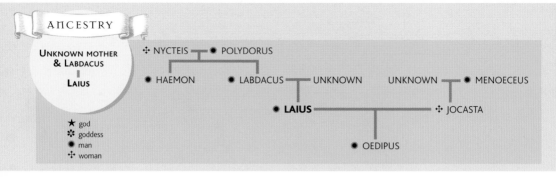

ANCESTRY

UNKNOWN MOTHER & LABDACUS
     |
LAIUS

✣ NYCTEIS ── ✸ POLYDORUS

✸ HAEMON   ✸ LABDACUS ── UNKNOWN   UNKNOWN ── ✸ MENOECEUS

✸ **LAIUS** ──────────────── ✣ JOCASTA

✸ OEDIPUS

★ god
✸ goddess
✸ man
✣ woman

L A I U S

King of Thebes and father of Oedipus.

Warned by the Oracle at Delphi that a future son would kill him, Laius took the precaution of abstaining from sexual relations with his wife Jocasta so that she would not become pregnant. However, unhappy at her husband's rejection of her, Jocasta plied the king with drink one night and induced him to sleep with her. The result was the conception of Oedipus. After the baby was born, in a bid to rid himself of the potential assassin, Laius had the infant taken to Mount Cithaeron, where he was left to die of exposure. However, a shepherd found him and gave him to the childless Polybus, king of Corinth, who adopted the boy and brought him up.

DEATH ON THE ROAD

Oedipus met his father by chance, many years later, although they were unaware of their relationship. Laius was on his way to Delphi to ask the Oracle for advice about how to deal with the monster Sphinx, which was plaguing his kingdom as a punishment for his sexual misdemeanor with a pupil. As king, he was traveling in a chariot along a narrow mountain track, and he ordered Oedipus, who was on foot, to move aside to allow the royal party to pass. Oedipus replied that he knew no one better than the gods or his parents. Laius was incensed at the young man's impudence and ordered his charioteer to ride on. A wheel ran over Oedipus' foot and a fight ensued in which the king was killed, slain by his own son, thus fulfilling the Oracle's prophecy.

Later, when a plague descended on Thebes, the Oracle pronounced the cause to be the presence in their midst of Laius' murderer. Oedipus, having now succeeded his father to the throne, proclaimed that the murderer should be expelled. When it was revealed by a blind seer, Tiresias, that Oedipus was really Laius' son, the fateful king was driven out of the city and forced to live in exile.

UNWITTING PATRICIDE
A Roman fresco showing Laius being killed unwittingly by Oedipus, his estranged son.

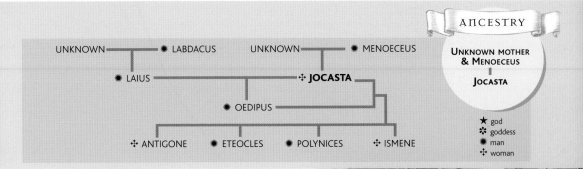

UNKNOWN	LABDACUS	UNKNOWN	MENOECEUS
LAIUS		✤ JOCASTA	

OEDIPUS

✤ ANTIGONE ❋ ETEOCLES ❋ POLYNICES ✤ ISMENE

★ god
❋ goddess
❋ man
✤ woman

JOCASTA

*Wife of Laius, king of
Thebes, and mother of
Oedipus.*

The tragic story of Jocasta
began when her
husband, King Laius,
turned against her because she
was unable to bear him a son.
When the king consulted the
Delphic Oracle for advice,
however, he was told that being
childless was a blessing, for any
son he might have would kill
him. The king, therefore, was no
longer interested in having sexual
relations with his wife for fear
that she might become pregnant.
Insulted by her husband's
rejection of her, Jocasta plied the
king with wine one night to
arouse his ardor. After succeeding
in her ploy, she became pregnant
and gave birth to a son, later
named Oedipus. Anxious for his
own future, Laius snatched the
baby away at birth and
abandoned him on Mount
Cithaeron. The Fates saved
Oedipus who was adopted and
brought up Polybus, king of
Corinth. Later, as foretold by the
Oracle, Laius perished before his
time, killed unwittingly by his
own son in an argument.

When Oedipus was
crowned king of
Thebes, after solving
the riddle of the
Sphinx, he married
Jocasta as his queen,
although neither
were aware of their
true relationship. It
was the blind seer
Tiresias who
announced to all at
Thebes that Jocasta
had married her son.
When incest was
confirmed in a letter
detailing the history of
Oedipus' adoption by
Polybus, Jocasta was so
mortified that she
took her own life.

One tradition says that
Jocasta's brother Creon expelled
King Oedipus from the city,
while others say that the Fates
so tormented him that he was
forced into exile.

Jocasta was the chief
priestess of the Sphinx, who
would set its trapped victims
a riddle to answer. If anyone
gave the correct answer, the
Sphinx was obliged to commit
suicide, which was also Jocasta's
destiny. The manner of Jocasta's
death is uncertain. By tradition
she hanged herself, but more
probably, Jocasta, like the Sphinx

THE CASE OF JOCASTA
*An illustration from a 15th-century
manuscript, which shows Oedipus
blinding himself and Jocasta looking
downcast after finding out the whole
truth of their relationship. The man
in the middle with the red stockings
is probably Tiresias.*

who flung herself off Mount
Phicium, jumped from a
high rock.

ANCESTRY

CHARICLO & EVERES

TIRESIAS

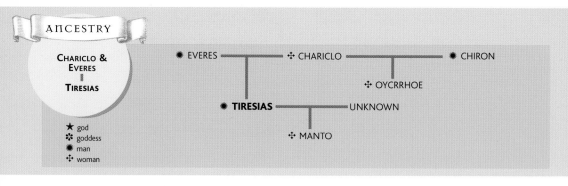

★ god
✤ goddess
✳ man
✤ woman

TIRESIAS

Renowned blind seer from Thebes.

Traditions disagree on how Tiresias came to lose his sight. One myth says that he was blinded by the goddess Athena when he saw her bathing nude. Then, in response to his mother's plea, the goddess sympathized and gave him the gift of prophecy as compensation.

Another myth says that Tiresias settled a dispute between Zeus and his wife Hera. She was complaining about his numerous infidelities and Zeus defended himself by saying that when they lay together she enjoyed it more than he did because women enjoy sexual pleasures far more than men. When Teresias was asked for his opinion, he said that a woman's pleasure in sexual intercourse was nine times greater than a man's. Hera was so furious at his answer that she blinded him for agreeing with Zeus, who rewarded Tiresias with a long life and the power of prophecy.

As a seer, Tiresias foretold the gods' will at Oedipus' court on a number of occasions, including the onset and cessation of plagues that were sent to the city. He also revealed to Jocasta the dreadful truth that her husband Oedipus was in fact her son.

WISDOM IN THE UNDERWORLD

Tiresias died after drinking from a spring, but lost none of his wisdom in death. When Odysseus visited the Underworld to seek Tiresias' advice about his return journey to Ithaca, the witch Circe told him that neither Hades nor Persephone had been able to dull the seer's inner vision. She noted, "For though he is dead, he alone has a mind to reason with. The rest are mere shadows flitting to and fro." On reaching the edge of the Underworld, Odysseus performed rites to attract Tiresias, cutting the throats of sheep over a trench to collect their blood, and sitting on guard, sword in hand, to keep away feckless ghosts before Tiresias appeared to him.

ODYSSEUS INVOKES TIRESIAS
Odysseus is shown here trying to attract Tiresias in the Underworld.

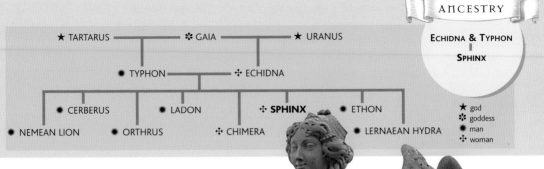

★ TARTARUS ———— ✤ GAIA ———— ★ URANUS

✷ TYPHON ———— ✤ ECHIDNA

✷ CERBERUS   ✷ LADON   ✤ SPHINX   ✷ ETHON

✷ NEMEAN LION   ✷ ORTHRUS   ✤ CHIMERA   ✷ LERNAEAN HYDRA

★ god
✤ goddess
✷ man
✤ woman

SPHINX

A fabulous creature with wings, a woman's head, and a lion's body.

This daughter of the many-headed monster Typhon and the serpent Echidna was sent by the goddess Hera to plague the city of Thebes in Boeotia. The inhabitants were to be punished for Laius' abduction of a boy, Chrysippus, son of Pelops. Another version of the myth says that Apollo sent the Sphinx as a punishment because the people of Thebes had neglected to carry out their duties with regard to the rituals of the gods.

The Sphinx had flown to Thebes from Ethiopia and dwelled in a rocky place, preying on travelers and challenging them to answer a riddle taught by the Muses: "What is the animal that has four feet in the morning, two feet at midday, and three feet at sunset?" As long as no one was able to solve the riddle, the plague on Thebes continued. Those who gave the wrong answer were immediately throttled by the Sphinx (the name in Greek means

FANTASTIC BEAST
The Sphinx is envisaged as a fearsome combination of lion, woman, and wings.

"strangler") and devoured. One of these victims was Jocasta's nephew Haemon (whose name in Greek is close to the word for "bloody").

Oedipus was the first person to guess the answer correctly, which was "man," who is at first a baby on all fours, then walks upright, and, when he is old, leans on a stick as a third foot. As soon as the Sphinx heard that Oedipus had answered her riddle, she threw herself into a chasm, killing herself. The inhabitants of Thebes were overjoyed at being released from the beast's power, and made Oedipus their king.

THEBAN GODDESS

The Sphinx is said to have originated in ancient Egypt and came to Greece via the Near East. She may have played a role as the local goddess in Thebes, the two animal parts of her body representing two halves of the year. The lion element marks the growing season and the serpent marks the year's decline. The king had to make his offerings before marrying the priestess—in this case, respectively Laius and Jocasta.

THE
TROJAN WAR

THE TROJANS

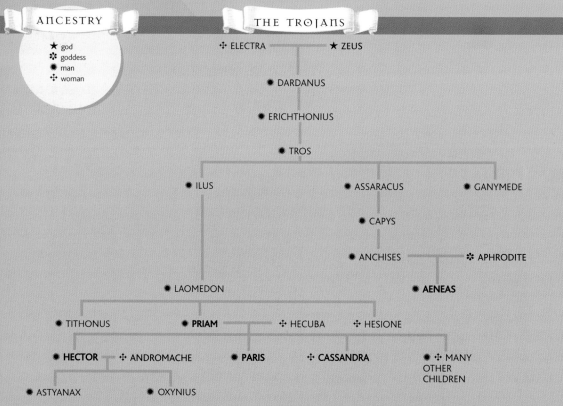

Ancestry legend:
- ★ god
- ❋ goddess
- ✷ man
- ✛ woman

Family tree:

- ✛ ELECTRA — ★ ZEUS
  - ✷ DARDANUS
    - ✷ ERICHTHONIUS
      - ✷ TROS
        - ✷ ILUS
        - ✷ ASSARACUS
          - ✷ CAPYS
            - ✷ ANCHISES — ❋ APHRODITE
              - ✷ **AENEAS**
        - ✷ GANYMEDE
        - ✷ LAOMEDON
          - ✷ TITHONUS
          - ✷ **PRIAM** — ✛ HECUBA
          - ✛ HESIONE
            - ✷ **HECTOR** — ✛ ANDROMACHE
              - ✷ ASTYANAX
              - ✷ OXYNIUS
            - ✷ **PARIS**
            - ✛ **CASSANDRA**
            - ✷✛ MANY OTHER CHILDREN

The ten-year war between the Greeks and Trojans was sparked by the gift from Aphrodite of the beautiful Greek Helen to the Trojan warrior Paris. Helen's husband Menelaus and the Greek army led by Agamemnon sailed to reclaim her. The trick of the wooden Trojan horse finally resulted in the fall of Troy. The chapter also includes the aftermath of the war and the affairs of the Trojan warrior Aeneas, who later founded the colony in Italy, from which the Romans trace their origins.

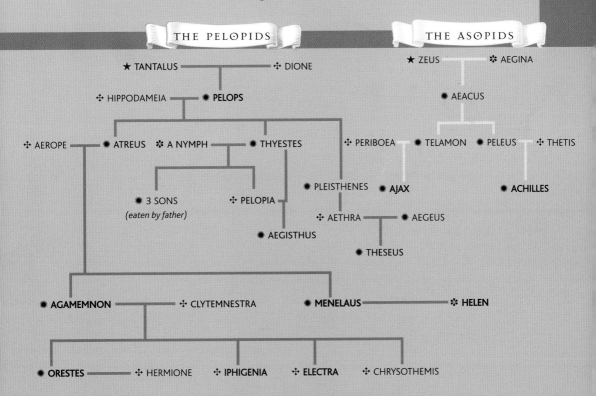

PARIS

*Son of King Priam of Troy; carried off Helen and started the
Trojan War; sometimes known as Alexander.*

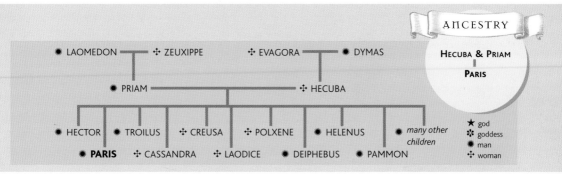

★ god
❈ goddess
★ man
✤ woman

★ LAOMEDON — ✤ ZEUXIPPE   ✤ EVAGORA — ★ DYMAS

★ PRIAM — ✤ HECUBA

★ HECTOR ★ TROILUS ✤ CREUSA ✤ POLXENE ★ HELENUS *many other children*

★ PARIS ✤ CASSANDRA ✤ LAODICE ★ DEIPHEBUS ★ PAMMON

It was prophesied to King Priam that his son would bring about the fall of his city, Troy. As a result, the child, Paris, was abandoned on a mountain to die. However, he was found on the hillside and raised by shepherds.

THE JUDGMENT OF PARIS

When Paris returned to Troy as a young man, Zeus instructed the messenger god Hermes to ask him to judge who was the fairest of the goddesses, Aphrodite, Athena, or Hera. Mischievous Eris had thrown a golden apple on the ground as the prize. Paris insisted on judging them in turn and naked. Hera turned her wonderful figure slowly before him and promised to make him lord of all Asia. Athena went further still and promised to make him victorious in all battles, as well as the most handsome and wise man in the world. But knowing his humble upbringing, Paris countered that he was a shepherd at heart, not a soldier, and his father's kingdom was peaceful. Then the lovely Aphrodite turned on her charm and promised him a woman as beautiful as she was, and Paris declared her the winner. She took Paris to Sparta to woo Helen, the beautiful wife of Menelaus.

INTO WAR

When the Spartan ruler Menelaus was abroad, Paris seduced Helen, and they eloped first to the island of Cranae and thence to Troy, so provoking the Trojan War. During the siege of Troy, Apollo guided the arm of Paris so that his poisonous arrow struck Achilles fatally on his right heel, his one vulnerable spot, causing the Greek soldier to die in agony.

FATAL WOUNDS

One of the boldest of the Greek fighters, Philoctetes, also one of Helen's suitors before her marriage to Menelaus, was sent by Heracles to help in the sacking of Troy and, specifically, to kill Paris. He challenged the Trojan prince to a duel of archery. His arrows struck Paris on the bow-hand and eyes, blinding him, before he received a fatal wound on the ankle. Paris limped from the field of combat and begged his former mistress Oenone to treat him. Her jealous hatred of Helen at first made her refuse, but later she relented and hurried back to him with healing drugs. It was too late, however, as her doomed lover had already perished from his wounds.

THE GOLDEN APPLE OF HESPERIDES
Paris holds the prized golden apple, while each of the three goddesses try to persuade him to give it to her.

HELEN

In Greek mythology, Helen was the wife of Menelaus, King of Sparta.
She eloped with the Trojan prince Paris and thus caused the ten-year
war between the Greeks and the Trojans.

Helen was the daughter of Zeus and Leda, or possibly of Nemesis, the personification of retribution. She could have been an ancient goddess connected with vegetation. By the time of Homer, around the seventh century BC, she had become a woman whose beauty was so powerful that it brought death and destruction to the mortal world.

OATH OF TYNDAREUS

When Helen was ready to marry, suitors came from all over Hellas to seek her hand. Fearing that the rejected suitors would quarrel and start a war, Tyndareus, king of Sparta, insisted that all the suitors swear an oath to protect and defend whoever was chosen as Helen's husband against any wrong done to him. Tyndareus chose Menelaus, son of the king of Mycene and future king of Sparta, to be Helen's husband.

JUDGMENT OF PARIS

Helen's renowned beauty became established at a wedding. According to tradition, the mischievous Eris (the personification of Strife) threw a golden apple on the floor marked "For the most beautiful." Paris was asked to judge between the three goddesses Hera, Athena, and Aphrodite, who in turn offered him empire, military glory, and the most beautiful woman in the world (Helen). He chose Helen. The rejected Hera and Athena would later support the Greeks in the Trojan War.

TROJAN WAR

With the help of Aphrodite, the goddess of love, Paris persuaded Helen to desert her husband Menelaus and sail to Troy. The result was the invocation of the Oath of Tyndareus by Menelaus and his brother Agamemnon, and the commencement of the Trojan War.

Helen was torn between being the lover of a Trojan prince and the ex-wife of a Greek king. Homer's *Iliad* relates how news of a temporary truce between the two sides filled Helen's heart with tender longing for her former husband and the city she had left. After the fall of Troy, Helen and Menelaus were reconciled.

Something of the sanctity traditionally attached to Helen may have prevented Homer from attaching any personal blame to her in the epic. Evidence of the special status she seems to have enjoyed occurs in a legend about her stay in Egypt. This version of her elopement has the mythical king Proteus substitute a spirit in her shape as Paris' companion, while Helen remains hidden safely in a cave on the Egyptian shore. After the fall of Troy, Menelaus called to collect her, and thereafter she led a more settled life.

LEDA AND THE SWAN

In Greek mythology, Leda was a princess from Aetolia who was seduced by Zeus. To achieve his conquest, Zeus took the guise of a swan, and Leda laid an egg from which Helen was born. Another tradition claims that Helen hatched not from Leda's egg, but from an egg laid by Nemesis, who had taken the form of a goose to escape the clutches of Zeus. Nevertheless the wily god managed to catch her. The resulting egg was abandoned by Nemesis. A herdsman found it and gave it to Leda, who carefully laid the egg in a casket. When Helen emerged and Leda saw how beautiful she was, Leda claimed her as her own daughter. Later tradition affirmed that, because of her love for Zeus, Leda was the mother of Helen.

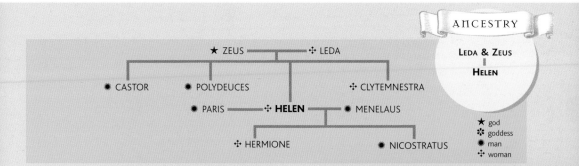

LEDA & ZEUS
|
HELEN

★ ZEUS ——— ✣ LEDA

✳ CASTOR   ✳ POLYDEUCES   ✣ CLYTEMNESTRA

✣ PARIS ——— ✣ **HELEN** ——— ✳ MENELAUS

✣ HERMIONE   ✳ NICOSTRATUS

★ god
✳ goddess
✳ man
✣ woman

IN LITERATURE

Both Plato, in the *Phaedrus*, and Euripides, in *Helen*, follow the variation of the story that it was a phantom, not Helen herself, that went to Troy. In Marlowe's play, *Doctor Faustus*, Helen's is "the face that launched a thousand ships." Her beauty and its short life are the subjects of many poems.

LEGENDARY BEAUTY
This white marble bust presents Helen as a classically beautiful woman.

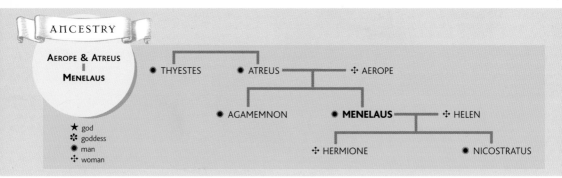

ANCESTRY

AEROPE & ATREUS
|
MENELAUS

★ THYESTES   ★ ATREUS ———— ✣ AEROPE

★ AGAMEMNON   **★ MENELAUS** ———— ✣ HELEN

✣ HERMIONE   ★ NICOSTRATUS

★ god
✤ goddess
★ man
✣ woman

MENELAUS

King of Sparta and husband of Helen.

While Menelaus was still a boy, Aegisthus killed his father Atreus, king of Mycenae. This deed was ordered by Atreus' brother Thyestes so that he could usurp the throne. Menelaus and his elder brother Agamemnon were brought up in Aetolia (western Greece). When they came of age, Tyndaseus led them back to Mycenae, and then forced Thyestes to relinquish his crown so that Agamemnon, the rightful heir, could become king of Mycenae. In time, Menelaus acceded to the throne of Sparta when Tyndareus abdicated.

First, however, he found a wife in Helen, daughter of Leda and Zeus.

TROPHY WIFE

Helen's beauty was renowned far and wide, and all the kings of Greece came to Sparta in a bid to secure her hand in marriage. Before her father made the final choice, he made all the suitors swear allegiance to whoever became Helen's husband, vowing that they would support him if he suffered any wrongdoing during the course of his marriage. Menelaus was then chosen as Helen's husband.

Eventually, therefore, when Menelaus, as king of Sparta, was deserted by Helen who eloped with Paris, all the kings of Greece rallied to his side and waged war on Troy to secure her return. Some traditions say that Helen was abducted by Paris against her will. Whether or not this was the case, Menelaus urged his brother Agamemnon to raise an army in her honor.

In the long war that ensued, Homer's *Iliad* relates how news of a temporary truce between the two sides filled Helen's heart with tender longing for her former husband. After the sack of Troy, Menelaus and Helen returned to Sparta, encountering many adventures on the way. The Spartan fleet suffered greatly because the gods of defeated Troy had not been appeased. Both the Trojan king Priam and Menelaus blamed the gods for the long conflict. The two leaders also blamed the arrogance and unscrupulous behavior of Paris, who had abused his position as an honored guest at the court of Sparta.

MENELAUS AND HELEN
Sixth-century BC vase showing the abduction of Helen from Menelaus.

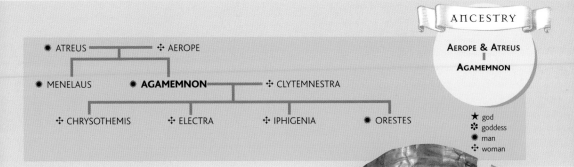

ATREUS — AEROPE

MENELAUS   **AGAMEMNON** — CLYTEMNESTRA

CHRYSOTHEMIS   ELECTRA   IPHIGENIA   ORESTES

★ god
❁ goddess
✹ man
✤ woman

AGAMEMNON

King of Mycenae and leader of the Greek expedition against Troy.

When Menelaus found that his wife Helen had been taken by Paris of Troy, he went to his brother Agamemnon in Mycenae and asked him to assemble a force to attack Troy. He sent heralds to each of the kings of Greece reminding them of the oaths they had sworn when Helen married Menelaus, obliging them to defend the betrayed husband's honor.

ASSAULT ON TROY

Agamemnon assembled a massive army at the port of Aulis in Boeotia, boarded on a thousand and thirteen ships. There was much confusion about the route to be taken to Troy which, together with adverse weather conditions, delayed their campaign by many years. When they finally departed on the right course, Agamemnon sent Menelaus and Odysseus ahead as envoys to demand the return of Helen from the Trojans. When these requests were rejected, Agamemnon set up camp on the island of Tenedos, a short distance across the sea from Troy.

The city was subjected to waves of onslaught by his finest Greek warriors, although many of his strategies were disputed by Achilles. Having penned in the Trojans, the Greeks beached their ships and besieged the city.

AFTERMATH OF TROY

Greeks soldiers were able to enter the city hidden inside a wooden horse. Having sacked the city, they seized the spoils of their conquest. As a special prize, Agamemnon took King Priam's daughter Cassandra as a concubine. After a quarrel with Menelaus over sacrifices to Athena, the victorious army set sail. Storms blew up and many ships were lost, as the gods exacted retribution on the Greeks for various offenses committed during the campaign.

When Agamemnon returned to Mycenae with Cassandra, Clytemnestra plotted the assassination of her husband, whom she now loathed. Agamemnon was a brutal man who stopped at nothing to get his own way. Not only did he kill

MYCENEAN MASK
This gold death mask was once thought to be of Agamemnon, but in fact it pre-dates the Trojan war.

Clytemnestra's former husband Tantalus and their child, but he forced her into marriage and then, while waiting for a fair wind on which to set sail, he permitted the sacrifice of Iphigenia, his own daughter.

Further complications arose when Clytemnestra took Agamemnon's cousin Aegisthus as a lover when Agamemnon was away at war. Aegisthus had killed his uncle Atreus, Agamemnon's father, while Agamemnon was an infant. Nervous about reprisals, Aegisthus assisted Clytemnestra in her husband's assassination by drowning him in his bath.

ACHILLES

*Hero of the Greek attack on Troy, son of Thessalian
king Peleus and sea nymph Thetis.*

Even before his birth, it was prophesied that Achilles would be greater than his father. For this reason, neither Zeus nor Poseidon dared to pursue the hero's beautiful mother Thetis. Instead, the cautious gods arranged for the sea nymph to marry a mortal ruler.

Thetis was not prepared to accept that Achilles would have to die, and she tried to endow him with immortality by various means. One way was dipping him as an infant into the river of Hades, the Styx, but since she had to hold him by the heel, this one spot was left unprotected. This vulnerability (known as the Achilles heel) allowed Paris to kill Achilles with a poisoned arrow.

CUNNING WARRIOR

Realizing that her son was destined to fall at the battle of Troy, Thetis did her utmost to prevent him from learning the arts of war, but nevertheless his prowess as a fighter became well known. Odysseus brought him to Agamemnon, king of Mycenae and leader of the Greek expedition against the Trojans. Although he owed no loyalty to Agamemnon, Achilles ignored his mother's advice and sailed with the fierce leader, taking with him his squire and lover Patroclus.

The fact that the southern Greeks needed Achilles, a northern prince, to bolster their expedition is an indication of the strength of his reputation as a fighter. When they were encamped before the mighty walls of Troy, the Greeks needed the power of Achilles, who commanded a ferocious army made up of the Myrmidons (meaning "ant-men," after Zeus had turned ants into soldiers). Yet he and Agamemnon clashed on many occasions, Achilles regarding the king as high-handed and ungrateful, and disagreeing with most of his

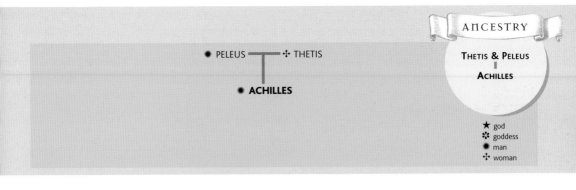

ANCESTRY

THETIS & PELEUS
|
ACHILLES

★ god
✳ goddess
✴ man
✛ woman

PELEUS ✴ — ✛ THETIS

✴ ACHILLES

strategies. Achilles was so stubborn in his opposition to Agamemnon that he refused all gestures of reconciliation, including his offer of marriage to any of his daughters. Taking his place, Patroclus put on the armor of his sulking lover and went out to help the Greeks. In the moment of triumph, however, Patroclus was killed by Hector,

the bravest son of the Trojan king, Priam.

SLAYING OF HECTOR

On hearing the news of Patroclus' death, Achilles was overcome by remorse. When Thetis came to mourn with him, he told his mother that he longed for death. He swore to avenge the death of his friend and thus

his fate was sealed. Clad in new armor made at Thetis' request by the smith god Hephaestus, Achilles sought out Hector, who stood his ground only after making the request that if he were killed, his body should be returned to King Priam. With rage undimmed, Achilles slew Hector, mutilated his body, and for twelve days dragged the bloody corpse behind his chariot around Patroclus' grave.

The death of Achilles himself was brought about by the sun god Apollo, when he guided Paris' arrow to penetrate the hero's vulnerable heel. The fearless warrior had earned the enmity of Apollo during the siege of Troy by killing several of his devoted followers, including his own son Tenes, king of the island of Tenedos.

DEATH OF HECTOR AND TRIUMPH OF ACHILLES
In revenge for the death of his lover, Patroclus, Achilles slays Hector in a scene set in the midst of battle.

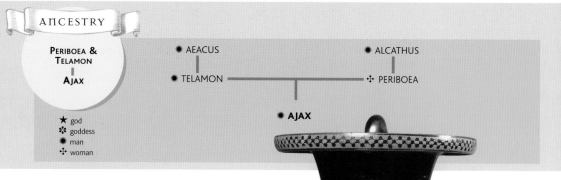

ANCESTRY

PERIBOEA &
TELAMON

AJAX

★ god
❉ goddess
✹ man
✛ woman

✹ AEACUS   ✹ ALCATHUS

✹ TELAMON ———————————— ✛ PERIBOEA

✹ AJAX

AJAX

Greek warrior in the siege of Troy.

Second only to Achilles in prowess as a warrior, Ajax was one of the key figures in the Greek war against Troy. He commanded 12 ships in the expedition led by Agamemnon, and was such a dedicated fighter that his contingent of warriors always stood out on the battlefield. Wherever danger threatened, there fought Ajax and his men. His size certainly helped—he possessed a huge head and shoulders, and towered above everyone else. He may have been slow of speech in the councils of war, but everyone acknowledged his tremendous courage once battle commenced.

During the war, Ajax fought fiercely with Hector, the greatest Trojan warrior. However, night intervened before their duel ended, so the two men gave each other gifts and departed homeward. Ajax saved the life of Odysseus, rallied the Greeks when the Trojans attacked their camp, and brought back the body of Achilles when he fell victim to a poisoned arrow shot by Paris.

Ajax's own death—and the chief element in his myth—resulted from a competition for Achilles' armor. It was usual for the personal effects of a hero to be awarded to the winner of a contest or game held at the funeral. When Odysseus won the magnificent armor that the smith god Hephaestus had made for Achilles, Ajax became mad with envy at his loss of status and planned a night attack on his own allies. Luckily, the goddess Athena deceived him into slaughtering a flock of sheep instead. Realizing his terrible intention and deeply ashamed, Ajax fell on his sword and died.

AJAX AND ACHILLES PLAY DICE
Athena watches as the two heroes take a break from battle to relax, still holding spears and shields.

Although there are other accounts of Ajax's death, the most potent image is that of the once-trusted warrior broken by remorse at the realization of his ungovernable pride.

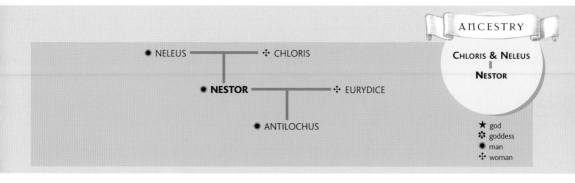

ANCESTRY

CHLORIS & NELEUS
|
NESTOR

NELEUS ━━━━━ ✣ CHLORIS

NESTOR ━━━━━ ✣ EURYDICE

ANTILOCHUS

★ god
✣ goddess
✴ man
✣ woman

NESTOR

Elder statesman of the ancient Greeks.

While still a child, Nestor's father and siblings were all killed by Heracles. As a young man, he showed his athleticism when he took part in the hunt of the violent Calydonian boar alongside Jason and Theseus. Fleet of foot, he outran the beast that gored and killed slower members of the party.

As the years went by, Nestor became renowned for his eloquence and wisdom. In preparation for the Trojan War, he helped Menelaus recruit leaders around Greece to take part in the expedition. Agamemnon sought his advice on military tactics. Nestor once advised the Greek commander-in-chief to send spies to Troy under cover of night to listen beneath the city walls to find out whom the Trojans feared most—Odysseus or Ajax.

Nestor ruled as king of Pylus in western Peloponnese for three generations by the favor of Apollo, and was said to have lived to a great age. He was into the third generation by the time of the Trojan War. The Greeks believed that it was Apollo who was responsible for taking the lives of Nestor's brothers and sisters, and that he gave the years to this old sage instead. Nestor managed to return safely home to Pylos from Troy because he left before Athena caused a great storm to blow up, which wrecked the ships of many other Greek leaders. He died quietly at Pylos.

Nestor's son Antilochus was one of Helen's suitors when the leaders of Greece were invited by Tyndareus to contend for her hand. But he perished in the war after coming to rescue his father, whose chariot horse had been shot by Paris.

BRISEIS BROUGHT TO ACHILLES BY NESTOR
This 1630 painting by Rubens depicts Nestor presenting Briseis, the beautiful daughter of Calchas, to Achilles during the Trojan War. Briseis was a trophy concubine earned by Achilles for capturing Trojan cities.

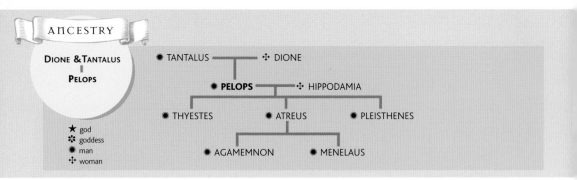

TANTALUS ——— ✤ **DIONE**

✹ **PELOPS** ——— ✤ **HIPPODAMIA**

✹ **THYESTES**   ✹ **ATREUS**   ✹ **PLEISTHENES**

✹ **AGAMEMNON**   ✹ **MENELAUS**

PELOPS

Son of Tantalus, king of Lydia, and founder of the Pelopid dynasty whose name was given to the Peloponnese region of Greece.

One of three sons of King Tantalus of Lydia, Pelops inherited much of his father's land and wealth, especially in Asia Minor. But wars with neighbors, including King Ilus of Troy, forced him to emigrate. One tradition says that Poseidon gave him a golden chariot and a team of immortal horses to carry him, his retinue, and his treasures across the Aegean Sea. At Olympia he competed in a chariot race against Oenamaus, king of Pisa and Elis, so that he might win the ruler's daughter Hippodamia as a prize. To ensure that he was the victor, Pelops bribed the charioteer Myrtilus, a son of Hermes and reputedly the swiftest in the land, to remove the pins from the king's wheels.

CURSE ON THE HOUSE OF PELOPS

As the race reached its climax, the wheels of Oenomaus' chariot suddenly flew off, flinging its rider to his death as he was trampled beneath the horses' hooves. However, Pelops did not honor his agreement with Myrtilus and pay him what was due, but pushed him into the sea instead. As Myrtilus was drowning, he cursed Pelops and his descendants for generations to come.

In search of purification after his murderous deed, Pelops drove his magic chariot across the western sea and was cleansed by Hephaestus. Afterward, he returned to his own country and laid claim to Oenomaus' throne. Thereafter, he succeeded in subjugating the entire region of what is now known as the Peloponnese. He even built a temple to Hermes in an attempt to atone for the loss of the god's son. However, a ghost, known as the horse-scarer, arose to haunt his house for generations to come. The curse afflicted the life of Pelops' son Atreus and his sons Agamemnon and Menelaus, who fought the ten-year Trojan War.

RACING FOR THE HAND OF HIPPODAMIA
Preparations for the chariot race between Pelops and Oenomaus.

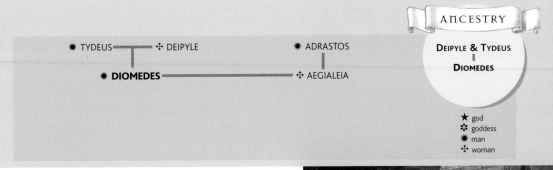

TYDEUS — DEIPYLE   ADRASTOS

DIOMEDES ————————————— AEGIALEIA

★ god
❋ goddess
✸ man
✣ woman

DIOMEDES

Greek king and warrior at the siege of Troy.

Renowned for his bravery, Diomedes figured among the fifty warriors who entered Troy inside the wooden horse. He was renowned for heroic deeds in combat and was a great athlete, winning the Greek games at chariot-racing and running.

After his marriage to Aegialeia, daughter of Adrastos, Diomedes battled courageously in the expedition against Thebes. But it was in the campaign against Troy that he earned his fame as an outstanding fighter. He was engaged on espionage sorties into the Trojan hinterland, surviving on his wits and alacrity; and in the absence of Achilles, led an onslaught on Troy.

After ten years of war, when Greek morale was low, it was Diomedes who accompanied Odysseus on the trip to Lemnos to retrieve Heracles' bow. (Other accounts say they fetched the archer Philoktetes). Calchas, the seer, had prophesied that the Greeks would not defeat Troy without first acquiring this bow. Successful in their quest,

Diomedes again assisted Odysseus, this time in stealing the sacred Palladium of Athena from within the precincts of Troy and dispatching it to the Greek ships waiting in the harbor.

TROJAN HORSE

When the time came for the wooden horse to be presented as a spurious gift for the Trojans, Diomedes climbed inside and waited silently for the assault. When the enemy was asleep, Odysseus opened a hatch on the underside of the horse, releasing the warriors, who silently slid to the ground. Diomedes and the other warriors made their way to the walls and opened up the gates, allowing in their own forces waiting outside. The Trojans were massacred in their sleep. Helen was found and taken to the waiting Greek ships while the city burned. After the

EATEN BY HIS OWN HORSES
One of Heracles' labors was to steal Diomedes' four man-eating horses. After his lover was eaten by the horses, Heracles set the horses on Diomedes himself.

sack of Troy, Diomedes was one of the few Greeks to have a safe and speedy voyage home.

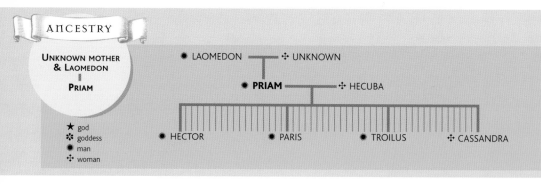

UNKNOWN MOTHER
& LAOMEDON

PRIAM

★ god
❋ goddess
✷ man
✛ woman

✷ LAOMEDON ——— ✛ UNKNOWN

✷ PRIAM ——— ✛ HECUBA

✷ HECTOR   ✷ PARIS   ✷ TROILUS   ✛ CASSANDRA

PRIAM

Aged king of Troy at the time of the Trojan War.

The fatal conflict between the Greeks and Trojans was in part caused by the ingratitude of Laomendon, Priam's father, to Apollo and Poseidon. He refused to pay these gods the money he owed them for building the walls of Troy. In revenge, Poseidon helped the Greeks during their ten-year siege of the city, and did not rest until the city was sacked.

Priam was an honest ruler and brought prosperity to his city. His wife was Hecuba, a Phrygian princess, and he had fifty sons (not all by Hecuba), the most famous being Hector, Paris, and Troilus. His daughter Cassandra foretold the fall of Troy, but Apollo, having taught her the art of fortune-telling, had ensured that her prophecies would never be believed.

The chief myths surrounding Priam are to be found in Homer's *Iliad*, the epic story of the Trojan War. There he is shown as a kind and thoughtful king, whose honesty was acknowledged even by the Greek warriors. The Greeks also admired Priam's courage in coming to Achilles to claim Hector's body, after his son had been killed in single combat with the Greek champion. Priam's fate was that his city should be brought to ruin by his son, Paris, who eloped with Helen, wife of the Spartan king Menelaus. Aphrodite, goddess of love, aided Paris in his seduction of Helen, but it soon became clear to Priam that many deities were giving direct aid to the Greek expedition sent to rescue the Spartan queen. Helen's own sympathies during the long war were somewhat ambiguous, but the king always showed her kindness.

Priam perished during the fall of Troy, killed by Pyrrhus, son of Achilles.

THE SACK OF TROY
Priam, father of Paris and Hector, is slain by Pyrrhus, a son of Achilles, during the sack of Troy.

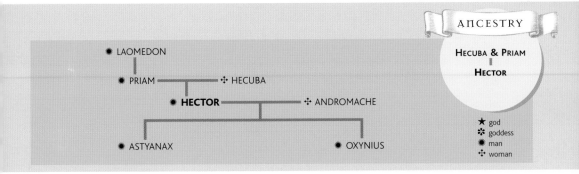

LAOMEDON

PRIAM ——— ❖ HECUBA

HECTOR ——————— ❖ ANDROMACHE

ASTYANAX   OXYNIUS

★ god
❉ goddess
✳ man
❖ woman

HECTOR

Son of Priam and Hecuba, Hector was the greatest of the Trojan warriors.

As commander of the Trojan army, it was Hector who led the storming of the Greek battlements where they encamped. Only Zeus' intervention saved the Greeks, who were pushed back to their ships. At this point, Achilles' lover Patroclus engaged Hector in a duel, but was killed in the fight after the god Apollo supported Hector. The victor then took Achilles' armor (which Patroclus was wearing) and put it on himself. Maddened with grief and fury, Achilles vowed to avenge his lover's death. In the ensuing battle, the terrifying Achilles and his warriors raged at the enemy, chasing them from the field of combat.

Only Hector remained, waiting for the ultimate duel. Thinking that he could outrun the weary Achilles, Hector turned and sped off. But Achilles gave chase around the city. As Hector's wife Andromache looked on from the walls of Troy, she beheld the warrior's breast pierced by Achilles' spear. As Hector lay dying, Apollo granted him the satisfaction of telling Achilles of his own impending death. The Greek warrior then mounted his chariot and ostentatiously dragged his victim's corpse around the walls of Troy and returned to his camp.

Although a lesser warrior than his counterpart Achilles, Hector was probably the better leader. He was not as proud and vengeful as Achilles, and was believed to be a virtuous man and a good husband and father, who knew that his people were doomed. He also knew about his own fate, but believed that as long as he was brave, he would die in glory. Hector's chivalry became a popular theme for later medieval writers.

ACHILLES' REVENGE
Achilles dragged his adversary Hector's body behind his chariot for 12 days.

AENEAS

Son of Aphrodite and a famous Trojan, adopted by the Romans as their national hero.

At the fall of Troy, Aeneas was said to have escaped the burning city with his wife Creusa, carrying his father Anchises on his back and leading his son Ascanius by the hand. At first, Anchises refused to abandon Troy, but two signs persuaded him to leave: a gigantic thunderbolt and a halo that appeared above Ascanius' head. During their flight, Creusa became separated from the party and disappeared. Eventually, Aeneas saw her ghost and learned from it that he would found a new state in Italy.

The long and indirect voyage to this final goal took Aeneas and his fellow fugitives to Thrace, Crete, North Africa, and Sicily. This zigzag course was caused by misinterpreting omens and oracles about where the new Troy should be established. Juno sent a great storm to destroy the fleet carrying the Trojan refugees who were forced to make for Carthage, where Juno caused Aeneas to fall in love with Dido, its queen. But despite Dido's legendary beauty, Aeneas obeyed the command of his destiny and set sail for Italy. Aboard the departing vessel, Aeneas saw flames rising from the pyre on which Dido was cremated—the distraught Carthaginian queen had committed suicide.

Thereafter, opposition from the goddess Juno (the Roman equivalent of Hera) could only slow the approach of Aeneas to his final destination. At Cumae, on the bay of Naples, Aeneas consulted the Sibyl, a revered and ancient prophetess, who directed him to find the entrance to the Underworld. There he saw the ghost of his father who had died on the voyage to Carthage. Learning from the ghost that Rome would eventually dominate the Mediterranean world, Aeneas and his followers moved north to Latium.

THE SIBYL

The Sibyl was a divinely inspired prophetess in both Greek and Roman mythology. There were as many as ten Sibyls and their oracles were in widely separated parts of the Mediterranean world. The most famous Roman prophetess was the Cumaean Sibyl, who escorted Aeneas to the Underworld. To gain admittance, he followed her orders by plucking the Golden Bough and making sacrifices to the gods.

The Sibyl then led him through the many realms of the Underworld: furthest the Fields filled with war heroes; the Fields of Mourning where, among others, those who had suffered an unjust fate resided. Among these latter souls was Dido, whom Aeneas pitied with a heavy heart. They came finally to the Elysian Fields, where Aeneas heard the music of Orpheus and met the ghost of his father Anchises. He revealed to his son how the universe worked and how some who died would return to earth after a thousand years with no memory of their previous lives.

SIBYL AS PROPHETESS
The Sibyl guided heroes, including Aeneas, through prophecies.

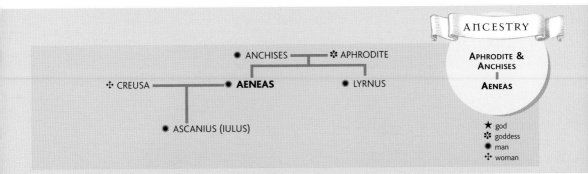

* ANCHISES ❊ APHRODITE

✢ CREUSA ✳ **AENEAS** ❊ LYRNUS

* ASCANIUS (IULUS)

**APHRODITE &
ANCHISES**

AENEAS

★ god
❊ goddess
✳ man
✢ woman

AENEAS FLEES TROY
*Carrying his father on his shoulder, Aeneas flees the burning Troy
with his wife and son to found a new state in Italy.*

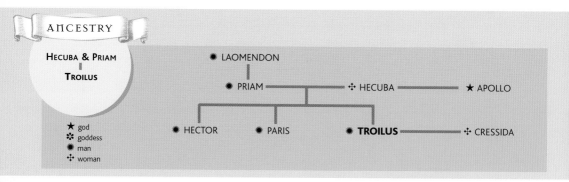

ANCESTRY

HECUBA & PRIAM
|
TROILUS

LAOMENDON

PRIAM ———————— HECUBA ———————— APOLLO

★ god
❋ goddess
✳ man
✣ woman

HECTOR   PARIS   TROILUS ———————— CRESSIDA

TROILUS

Officially son of King Priam of Troy but fathered by the god Apollo.

Troy was fated to fall to the Greeks if Troilus did not reach the age of twenty years. Some traditions say that Achilles fell in love with him as they fought, and that the youth fled and took refuge in the temple of Apollo. But when Achilles found him, the enraged Greek warrior beheaded Troilus, aged only nineteen years.

Another legend says that Troilus sought revenge on Achilles for the death of Memnon but died in combat, or was taken prisoner and then slaughtered on Achilles' orders. However he died, Troilus was killed by Achilles.

TROILUS AND CRESSIDA
The story of Troilus' love for Chryseis (in Latin, Cressida) became popular in the Middle Ages, although it was a confusion of the Greek myth. In Greek mythology Troilus is said to have loved Briseis, a Trojan widow. But in medieval legend, he loves the beautiful daughter of the seer Calchas. As the legend developed, Briseis came to be identified with Chryseis, or Cressida. When her father Calchas defected to the Greek camp, he left his daughter behind in Troy. When she was exchanged for a Trojan prisoner of war, Cressida swore to remain faithful to Troilus, whom she loved. But once she settled with the Greeks, she fell in love with Diomedes, who tried to kill Troilus whenever he saw him on the battlefield. To end his sorrow, Troilus died willingly in the fray.

IN LITERATURE
Chaucer developed the legend of the two lovers, which was then used by Shakespeare in his play *Troilus and Cressida*. From then on, Cressida's name came to symbolize infidelity.

TROILUS ON HORSEBACK
In this 6th-century BC Etruscan fresco, Troilus is riding bareback, armed with a spear.

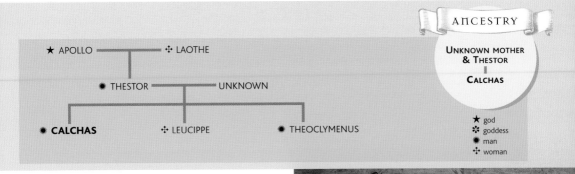

UNKNOWN MOTHER & THESTOR
|
CALCHAS

★ APOLLO ——— ✣ LAOTHE

✶ THESTOR ——— UNKNOWN

✶ CALCHAS   ✣ LEUCIPPE   ✶ THEOCLYMENUS

★ god
✶ goddess
✶ man
✣ woman

CALCHAS

Priest of Apollo and seer during the Trojan War.

This wise seer uttered many prophecies to Greeks during the Trojan War. Calchas spoke of many things that were incumbent on the Greek army if they were to gain the favor of the gods. In most cases, the will of the gods could be divined from signs in nature. On one occasion, a snake darted from under Apollo's altar and climbed a plane tree. There it attacked and swallowed eight sparrow chicks as well as its mother, then turned to stone. Calchas interpreted this as a sign from Zeus that each bird represented one year of war, so the Greeks would take Troy in the tenth year.

The most dreadful prophecy that Calchas had to deliver was one uttered to the Greek commander-in-chief, Agamemnon, an obligation of crushing magnitude. While his fleet waited at Aulis for better conditions to sail to Troy, the seer announced that only by appeasing Artemis would his ships be granted a favorable wind, and that appeasement could be bought only with the sacrifice of Iphigenia, Agamemnon's most beautiful daughter.

When the war had lasted nearly ten years and the Greeks were becoming demoralized, Calchas foretold that in order to capture Troy they would require Heracles' bow, and so Odysseus and Diomedes fetched its owner Philoctetes from the island of Lemnos. Calchas also helped Odysseus discover the secret of how to capture impregnable Troy. Three conditions first had to be met: the bones of Pelops had to be brought to the Greeks; Pyrrhus, son of Achilles, had to join the fray; and the Palladium of Athena had to be stolen from Troy. This statue, dedicated to Pallas Athena, was sacred and, while it remained

THE SACRIFICE OF IPHIGENIA
Calchas foretold that Artemis would only be appeased by the sacrifice of Agamemnon's daughter Iphigenia.

within the city walls, assured the safety of Troy.

Once all three tasks had been fulfilled, the city of Troy was rendered vulnerable—hence it fell afoul of the trick of the wooden horse. After the Trojan War, the seer was said to have died of mortification after losing a contest with another diviner, Mopsus, who proved his superiority in the art.

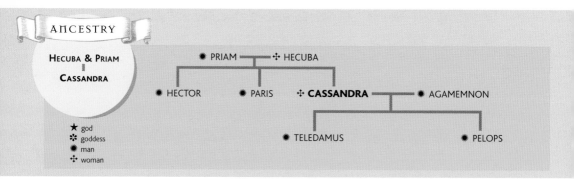

ANCESTRY

HECUBA & PRIAM
|
CASSANDRA

PRIAM — HECUBA

HECTOR   PARIS   CASSANDRA — AGAMEMNON

TELEDAMUS   PELOPS

★ god
✳ goddess
✻ man
✢ woman

CASSANDRA

Most beautiful of the daughters of the Trojan king and queen, Priam and Hecuba.

Several warriors became allies of the Trojans and fought to save the city from the Greeks during the Trojan War in the hope of being rewarded with Cassandra's hand in marriage. Such were her looks that, even as a child when she slept in the temple of Apollo, the god fell deeply in love with her and endowed the beautiful young girl with the gift of prophecy. In the morning when she awoke, Cassandra was discovered with numerous snakes that passed on secret knowledge by licking her ears.

When Cassandra had grown into a young woman, Apollo tried to claim her for himself. He was shocked to discover that she wished to remain chaste and she refused to believe that she owed him any gratitude for the gift of prophecy he endowed upon her. She agreed to give Apollo a kiss, whereupon his breath removed any credulity she had with others. Indeed, Cassandra, who went into a trance whenever she was receiving the foreknowledge of prophecy, was thought to be mad.

Cassandra foretold the harm that Paris would bring to Troy by eloping with Helen, but her words went unheeded. Most dramatic of all was her warning about the wooden horse, the device conceived by Odysseus to gain entry into Troy. Even though the armor of the Greek warriors hidden inside its belly was heard clashing loudly, Apollo made sure that Cassandra's warnings were ignored.

After the fall of Troy, the distraught prophetess was raped by the Greek warrior Ajax of Locris. He dared to commit this outrage in the temple of Athena. During the struggle, the goddess' sacred statue was overturned, a sacrilege for which Ajax and other Greeks suffered on their return journey, as Athena punished them with death.

Cassandra was awarded as a prize of war to Agamemnon, leader of the Greeks, and as his concubine she bore him two sons, Teledamus and Pelops. He took her back to his home in Mycenae, where she was killed by his vengeful wife Clytemnestra. Immediately before the event, Cassandra stood outside the palace and foretold her own fate and that of Agamemnon, who would become the victim of an assassination plot.

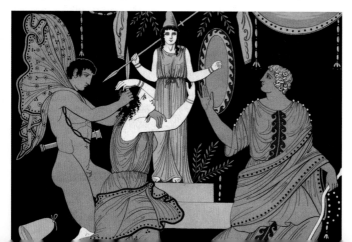

THE RAPE OF CASSANDRA
Ajax of Locris attacked Cassandra in the temple of Athena and knocked over the statue of the goddess.

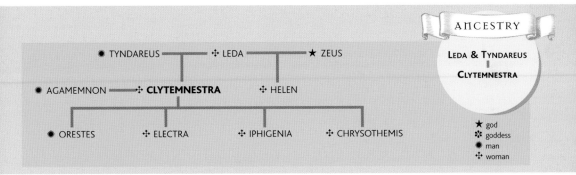

TYNDAREUS — LEDA — ZEUS

AGAMEMNON — **CLYTEMNESTRA**   HELEN

ORESTES   ELECTRA   IPHIGENIA   CHRYSOTHEMIS

★ god
❋ goddess
✹ man
✣ woman

CLYTEMNESTRA

Wife of Agamemnon and lover of Aegisthus.

MURDER OF CASSANDRA
A jealous Clytemnestra is depicted in the act of killing Cassandra.

Clytemnestra did not have a happy marriage, having been forced to marry Agamemnon after the warrior king of Mycenae had killed her first husband, Tantalus, king of Pisa, in battle. As the daughter of a high-ranking king, Tyndareus of Sparta, Agamemnon felt obliged to seek his forgiveness, which was granted. With Agamemnon, she bore four children: a son, Orestes, and three daughters, Electra, Iphigenia, and Chrysothemis. But Clytemnestra's woes continued when Agamemnon deceived her into sending Iphegenia to Artemis, supposedly to marry Achilles before he set off with the expeditionary fleet to Troy. Instead, the young girl was sacrificed on the altar of Artemis in order to obtain a favorable wind for sailing.

While Agamemnon spent ten years away from home warring with the Trojans, Clytemnestra took his cousin Aegisthus as a lover. When her warrior husband finally returned with his prize concubine, Cassandra, daughter of King Priam, she plotted his murder with Aegisthus. Appearing to greet her husband with affection, Clytemnestra led the battle-worn warrior to the bath-house for a long relaxing soak. When he stepped from the bath, she pretended that she was going to wrap him in a bath robe, but instead threw a net over his head, entangling him like a fish. Aegisthus emerged from the shadows and attacked Agamemnon with his sword, whereupon Clytemnestra delivered a vengeful blow with an axe, severing his head.

Crazed with jealousy and blood lust, Clytemnestra ran through the palace in search of Cassandra. Finding her outside in a trance, she used the same weapon to decapitate her husband's mistress. Meanwhile, Agamemnon's son Orestes was secreted away by his sister Electra to protect him from Aegisthus. Orestes later exacted a terrible price for these bloody acts, including the murder of his own mother.

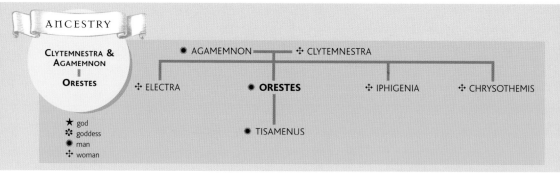

ORESTES

Son of Clytemnestra and Agamemnon, king of Mycenae; infamous for committing matricide.

While Agamemnon was leading the Greek war against Troy, his wife Clytemnestra took Aegisthus as a lover. Her motive may have been revenge, for, in order to obtain a fair wind for his ships, Agamemnon had sacrificed their daughter Iphigenia to the goddess Artemis at Aulis, in Boeotia. The princess had been called there from Mycenae on the pretext that she was to marry Achilles.

On Agamemnon's return from Troy, Clytemnestra and Aegisthus murdered him in his bath. Orestes was still a boy at the time and, to protect him, his sister Electra sent him to the court of a friendly king. There, Orestes grew up and became a warrior. When he asked the Oracle at Delphi about his father's murder, he was told to slay both Clytemnestra and her lover. Arriving secretly at Mycenae, Orestes made contact with Electra and plotted the deed.

AVENGING AGAMEMNON

Orestes arrived in disguise at the palace of Clytemnestra—who did not recognize him—and pretended to bear the sad news that her son was dead. Barely able to conceal her relief, she called the servants to fetch Aegisthus, who was outside. The unsuspecting paramour came in unarmed, and in one movement Orestes drew his sword and struck Aegisthus dead, thus avenging his father's murder. Despite her appeals for mercy, Orestes then cut off his mother's head with a single blow.

The legend of Orestes becomes even more complicated from then on, and there are several versions of subsequent events. Older traditions tend to accept the justice of his revenge, but later authors are less comfortable with the fact that Orestes murdered his mother. According to one version of the tale, Orestes was relentlessly pursued by the Furies as a punishment for matricide. Only when he had been acquitted by the court of Areopagus in Athens did they agree to stop pursuing him, and thereafter the Furies were known as the Eumenides—"Well-minded Ones."

IN LITERATURE

The modern writer Jean-Paul Sartre portrayed the plight of Orestes in his play *The Flies*.

ORESTES AND PYLADES
In this Roman fresco, Orestes (center) is shown returning to his home with his friend Pylades.

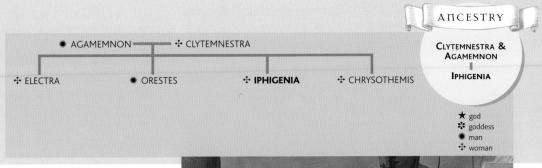

AGAMEMNON	CLYTEMNESTRA		
ELECTRA	ORESTES	IPHIGENIA	CHRYSOTHEMIS

★ god
✳ goddess
✴ man
✣ woman

IPHIGENIA

*Greek princess, daughter of
Agamemnon and Clytemnestra.*

When the Greek fleet was waiting to sail from Aulis to Troy, Artemis demanded the sacrifice of Iphigenia in return for a favorable wind. To appease the goddess for having upset her by boasting of being a better hunter, Agamemnon agreed and tricked Clytemnestra into bringing Iphigenia to Aulis on the pretext that she was to marry Achilles.

In some versions of the myth, the sacrifice was made; in others, Artemis substituted a hind for Iphigenia at the last moment and carried off Iphigenia, wrapped in a cloud, to Tauris in Crimea. There she served as high priestess at the shrine of Artemis. Subsequently, the Taurians identified her with the hunting goddess, although Iphigenia hated human sacrifice, one of the rituals of her cult.

SAVING ORESTES

Years later, Iphigenia's brother Orestes visited Tauris and was himself threatened with being sacrificed to Artemis when he appeared to be going mad. He knew nothing of Iphigenia's survival of the ordeal at Aulis, and, during the preparations for the ritual sacrifice of his life, they recognized each other. Desperate to save her brother, whom she loved despite the fact that he had murdered their mother, Iphigenia invented a story to deceive King Thoas of Tauris. He was anxious to proceed with the sacrifice, so she explained that the proposed victim was unfit for Artemis because he had committed

SACRIFICE OF IPHIGENIA
*Agamemnon prepares to sacrifice his
prettiest daughter Iphigenia to
appease Artemis.*

matricide. She claimed that she had to take Orestes, together with the image of Artemis, which had now been defiled by his gaze, to the sea to be purified. There they boarded a ship, and, with the help of Poseidon, who calmed the sea at the request of Athena, fled to safety in Greece.

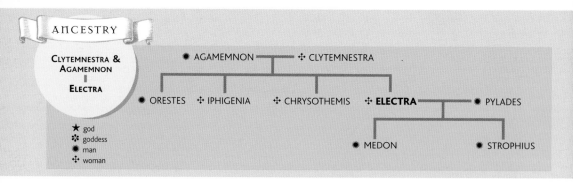

CLYTEMNESTRA & AGAMEMNON
|
ELECTRA

★ AGAMEMNON ——— ✢ CLYTEMNESTRA

★ ORESTES   ✢ IPHIGENIA   ✢ CHRYSOTHEMIS   ✢ **ELECTRA** ——— ★ PYLADES

★ god
✢ goddess
★ man
✢ woman

★ MEDON   ★ STROPHIUS

ELECTRA

Daughter of Agamemnon and Clytemnestra.

Much of the mythology about Electra (meaning "amber" in Greek) relates to her brother Orestes, whom she protected with an ardent, sisterly love. When their father Agamemnon, king of Mycenae, was murdered on his return from Troy by their mother Clytemnestra and her lover Aegisthus, Electra smuggled the young Orestes out of the city wrapped in a robe. He was then brought up safely in exile.

Electra was betrothed to marry her cousin Castor of Sparta, but Aegisthus, fearing that she might bear a son to avenge her father's murder, asserted his authority and announced that no suitor would be acceptable. Clytemnestra, however, was afraid of divine retribution and persuaded Aegisthus to allow her daughter to marry a Mycenaean peasant who was chaste. The marriage was never consummated and Electra lived in poverty with the ignominy of remaining childless, although she constantly reminded her brother of his moral duty to avenge their

father's death, in the hope that her circumstances might one day be changed.

When Orestes grew up, he secretly visited his father's tomb and met Electra, who was there offering prayers to the god Hermes. Some slave women who were mourning at the tomb revealed a recent nightmare of Clytemnestra in which she had given birth to a serpent which then suckled at her breast and drew blood instead of milk. Orestes inferred from the dream that he was the serpent. With Electra's help, he plotted his vengeance and duly killed both Clytemnestra and Aegisthus.

No longer constrained by their guarding influence, Electra was free to find a suitable husband for the purpose of bearing children. She married Pylades, son of Strophius, and had two children, Medon and Strophius the Second.

ORESTES AND ELECTRA
Electra smuggled her younger brother to safety.

IN LITERATURE

For the Greek tragedians, Electra is the central figure in an arena of murder and revenge. Euripides' play *Electra* shows her to be obsessed with her hatred, her father, and finally overwhelmed by guilt and remorse. The psychoanalyst Sigmund Freud coined the name "Electra complex" as a definition of a woman's fixation on her father, together with jealousy of her mother.

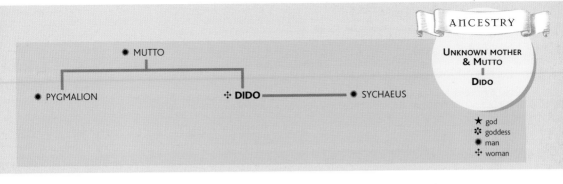

UNKNOWN MOTHER
& MUTTO

DIDO

★ god
❃ goddess
✳ man
✢ woman

MUTTO

PYGMALION   ✢ DIDO ——————— ✳ SYCHAEUS

DIDO

Legendary queen of Carthage to the Romans.

Dido was the daughter of Mutto, king of Tyre in Phoenicia, and the sister of Pygmalion. When the latter became king, he killed Dido's husband Sychaeus and she fled to Africa, where she founded and ruled over the city of Carthage.

When Aeneas' ship was driven by storms onto the coast at Carthage, Venus (Aphrodite), his mother, brought him and Dido together, and instructed Cupid to inspire them to become lovers. Although Dido had sworn never to remarry, she confided in her sister Anna that she was falling irresistibly in love with Aeneas. One day, as they were out hunting together, they took shelter from a sudden storm in a cave and made love. Despite the bliss they enjoyed, the tug of destiny drew Aeneas to Italy. At Jupiter's command, he knew he had no choice but to resume his duty to found Rome, and he planned his departure in secret. When Dido inadvertently discovered his intentions, she begged him to stay, but to no avail. Leaving the distraught Dido, he set sail. From the sea,

however, he was devastated to see the funeral pyre on which she had thrown herself in an act of suicide. Another version says that she preferred to burn herself to death rather than be married to a local king, Iarbus, who had sold her his land.

Even after her death Dido could not forgive Aeneas' desertion. When her lover descended to the Underworld to consult his father's ghost, she turned away and fled from him.

IN LITERATURE
Virgil's epic poem the *Aeneid* describes the story of Dido and Aeneas from the point of view of Roman sentiments regarding the primacy of patriotic duty. Later writers did not accept this. Both Chaucer, in *Legend of Good Women*, and Christopher Marlowe, in *Tragedy of Dido*, place more emphasis on Dido's heroism.

DEATH OF DIDO
Dido committed suicide when she was abandoned by Aeneas.

THE
ODYSSEY

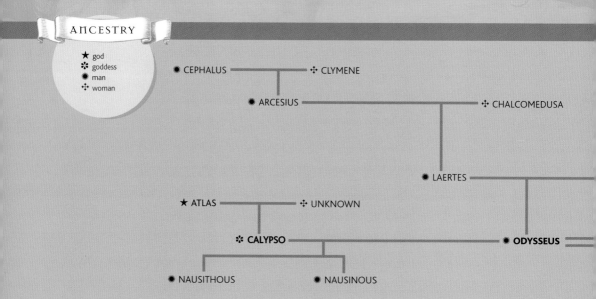

ANCESTRY

★ god
❋ goddess
✳ man
✛ woman

✳ CEPHALUS ——————————— ✛ CLYMENE

✳ ARCESIUS ——————————— ✛ CHALCOMEDUSA

✳ LAERTES ———————

★ ATLAS ——————— ✛ UNKNOWN

❋ CALYPSO ——————————————— ✳ ODYSSEUS

✳ NAUSITHOUS   ✳ NAUSINOUS

It took Odysseus, the Greek hero who had invented the wooden Trojan horse, ten years to return home to Ithaca. This chapter covers the adventures and hazards that he and his trusty crew encountered on the way. These include a chance meeting with the sea-god Poseidon, a narrow escape from the menacing Sirens whose entrancing song lured unsuspecting crews on to the rocks, and a skirmish with Circe the witch. He also languished on a desert island with the beautiful nymph Calypso before he finally returned home to his wife Penelope.

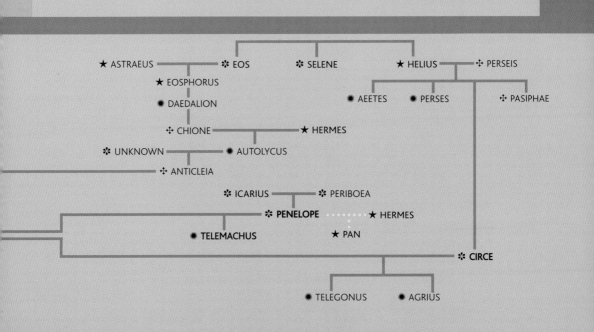

ODYSSEUS

Greek hero and king of Ithaca; known to the Romans as Ulysses.

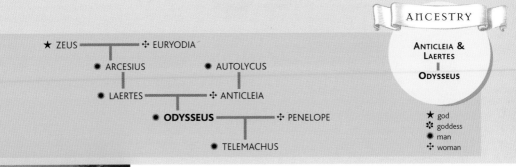

★ ZEUS ——— ✣ EURYODIA

✣ ANTICLEIA &
LAERTES

✳ ARCESIUS   **✳ AUTOLYCUS**

ODYSSEUS

✳ LAERTES ——— ✣ ANTICLEIA

★ god
✳ goddess
✳ man
✣ woman

✳ ODYSSEUS ——— ✣ PENELOPE

✳ TELEMACHUS

O dysseus has alternative genealogies. According to the Homeric epic, he was the son of Laertes. Another myth states that he was the illegitimate son of Sisyphus, founder of the city of Corinth. This would certainly account for his quick-wittedness, for Sisyphus was so intelligent that he successfully outwitted both Thanatos (Death) and the King of the Underworld, Hades.

Odysseus masterminded the Greek siege of Troy. He deceived the Trojans by introducing into their city, in the guise of a religious offering, a wooden horse filled with Greek soldiers. With this strategy, the Greeks were finally able to end the war.

Because Odysseus offended the sea god Poseidon by blinding the cyclopes Polyphemus, it was ten years before he could return home. Among the strange places he visited were the land of the Lotus-eaters (Lotophagi); the isle of the witch Circe, who tried to turn his crew into swine; the land of the cannibals (Laestrygonians);

ODYSSEUS AS BEGGAR
The goddess Athena helps Odysseus to disguise himself as a beggar on his return home.

the rocks occupied by the sweet-voiced Sirens; and the isle of the nymph Calypso. He also encountered Polyphemus, the one-eyed Cyclopes, on Sicily.

SLAUGHTERED SUITORS
Disguised as a beggar, Odysseus finally arrived at his palace where more than a hundred suitors waited on Penelope, his faithful wife. Since, after twenty years, she could presume herself to be a widow, she followed instructions left by Odysseus to choose a second husband. So Penelope promised to marry the suitor capable of bending a mighty bow that belonged to her husband. Odysseus. His son Telemachus stripped the hall of weapons and watched as each suitor in turn unsuccessfully attempted to string the bow. Then, to their astonishment, Odysseus, still in disguise, strung the bow, hit a target, and proceeded to massacre the suitors, aided only by two faithful herdsmen and Telemachus. Odysseus and Penelope were finally reunited.

The last years of Odysseus' life are uncertain. He either lived quietly with Penelope in Ithaca or, according to one legend, was condemned to exile for the revenge he had taken.

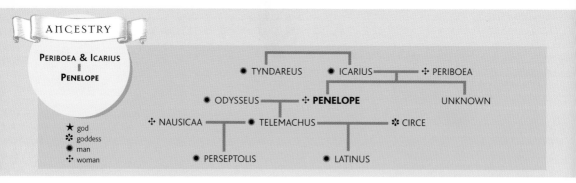

TYNDAREUS · ICARIUS —— PERIBOEA

ODYSSEUS —— PENELOPE   UNKNOWN

NAUSICAA —— TELEMACHUS —— CIRCE

PERSEPTOLIS   LATINUS

PENELOPE

Wife of Odysseus; she remained faithful during his twenty-year absence.

I n ancient Greece, Penelope became the symbol of wifely fidelity. She remained true to Odysseus, despite being left alone for ten years while he fought in the Trojan War and then another ten years while he made his long voyage home.

During his absence, Penelope managed their affairs in Ithaca, a small island in the Ionian Sea, and was beset by suitors. Eventually, she reluctantly agreed to choose another husband, but only when she had finished making her father-in-law's shroud. However, each night she unraveled what she had woven by day. When her ruse was uncovered by one of her maids, she promised to marry the hero who could bend Odysseus' bow and shoot an arrow through the holes in twelve axes lined up one in front of another. None could perform the feat, and the suitors agreed to postpone the trial. But a beggar among them asked if he might try his luck. When he succeeded in the trial, he threw off his disguise and revealed himself to be Penelope's long-awaited husband.

STRIPED DUCK

One myth describes how as a child, Penelope, who was then known as Arnacia, was thrown into the sea on her father's orders. A flock of purple-striped ducks buoyed her up, and sustained her, and eventually brought her ashore. Her parents, Icarius and Periboea, believing she was destined to survive, relented and gave her the new name of Penelope, meaning "duck."

WEAVING ON LOOM
Penelope used many tactics to avoid choosing a new suitor, including weaving a shroud by day and then unravelling it at night.

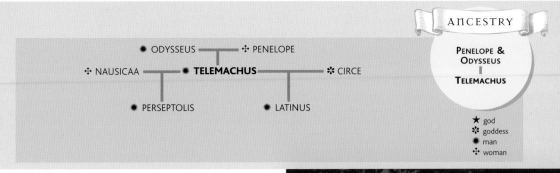

```
        ✴ ODYSSEUS ———— ✛ PENELOPE
                           |
  ✛ NAUSICAA ———— ✴ TELEMACHUS ———— ❋ CIRCE
              |                    |
      ✴ PERSEPTOLIS        ✴ LATINUS
```

★ god
❋ goddess
✴ man
✛ woman

TELEMACHUS

Son of Odysseus and Penelope.

Disguised as a friend of Odysseus, Athena appeared to Telemachus and entreated him to take control of the situation at the palace and expel the hundred or more suitors who were courting his mother, Penelope. Although Telemachus ordered them all to leave, they ignored his request. Athena also instructed him to discover the whereabouts of Odysseus, who had been absent for many years fighting in the Trojan War.

She provided him with a vessel and crew, and they sailed together to visit Nestor at Pylos. Although the old man had no news, he nevertheless directed Telemachus to Sparta, supplying him with a chariot and his own son Pisistratus as a guide. At Sparta, they asked Menelaus, the last of the Greeks to return home from Troy. He reported what he had heard from Proteus, the shepherd of sea creatures—namely, that Odysseus was still alive but held prisoner on an island belonging to the nymph Calypso.

While at Sparta, Athena appeared to Telemachus in a dream and warned him his mother's suitors were planning to ambush him on his return to Ithaca. After the end of Odysseus' long journey, father and son finally met again on their home island in the hut of Eumaeus, Odysseus' faithful swineherd. Before they entered the palace, they planned to kill Penelope's suitors.

Disguised as a beggar, Odysseus gained entry into the banquet hall, and, at a given moment, after shooting his bow, Odysseus threw off his disguise. Father and son, together with the help of two faithful herdsmen, then slaughtered all the suitors.

TELEMACHUS AND ODYSSEUS
Father and son reunited after Odysseus' twenty-year journey. Together they killed Penelope's suitors.

IN LITERATURE

In modern literature, Telemachus is characterized in James Joyce's novel *Ulysses* as Stephen Dedalus, who travels in search of his father.

ANCESTRY

THOOSA &
POSEIDON
|
POLYPHEMUS

★ god
✳ goddess
✴ man
✛ woman

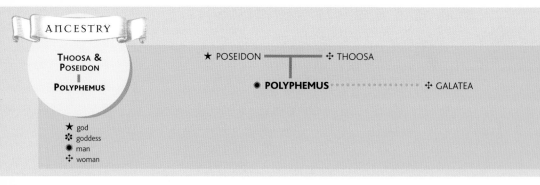

★ POSEIDON ——————— ✛ THOOSA

✴ POLYPHEMUS ············· ✛ GALATEA

POLYPHEMUS

A Cyclopes and shepherd son of Poseidon whom Odysseus encountered on his travels.

O f the two distinct groups of Cyclopes to appear in Greek mythology, one was made up of savage and lawless pastoralists from Sicily. One member, Polyphemus, the son of Poseidon and the nymph Thoosa, was a giant of a man with one eye. His favorite food was human flesh.

When the wanderer Odysseus visited Sicily, he went ashore with his crew and found a place to pitch camp. They had lit a fire and were feasting when Polyphemus appeared. He shepherded his flock into a cave and rolled a stone in front of it. He then noticed Odysseus and his companions. With merciless cruelty, the Cyclopes devoured six members of his crew, and was preparing to eat Odysseus last. In return for this courtesy, the voyager offered the giant some wine to help wash down his food. Polyphemus drank the wine, took more, and soon fell asleep in a drunken stupor.

Odysseus found a stake lying on the ground and, with his remaining four companions, sharpened one end, heated it up in the fire, and plunged it like a poker into Polyphemus' single eye, blinding him. To hide from the enraged giant, Odysseus spent the night among the sheep in Polyphemus' cave. When the flock left the cave the next morning, Odysseus clung to the underside of a large ram. The giant passed his hand along only the top of the creature, and so Odysseus escaped, unnoticed.

As the wanderer sailed away, he shouted to the Cyclops that he was Odysseus. Polyphemus had been warned by a seer that he would be blinded by Odysseus, and when he heard the name, the giant hurled huge boulders into the sea in anger. The ship escaped but Poseidon's anger was roused.

ODYSSEUS BLINDS POLYPHEMUS (DETAIL) *In order to escape from Polyphemus, Odysseus blinded him while he slept and then hid under the belly of a sheep.*

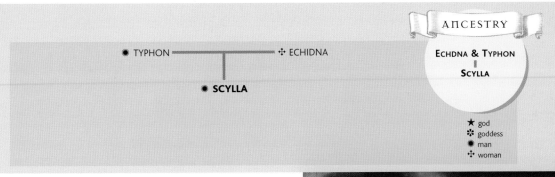

★ god
✲ goddess
✳ man
✥ woman

TYPHON ——— ✥ ECHIDNA

✳ SCYLLA

SCYLLA

A sea monster who lived in the Straits of Messina.

After Odysseus had survived the threat of the Sirens on his long journey home from the Trojan War, his ship passed between two cliffs along the Straits of Messina, the narrow passage of sea separating Italy from Sicily. One of the cliffs was home to Scylla, who was originally a beautiful nymph but who had been turned into a six-headed, dog-like monster. Her downfall began when she rejected the advances of the sea-god Glaucus, who then asked the enchantress Circe for a potion with which to win Scylla's love. Instead, Circe fell in love with Glaucus and, in a jealous rage, poisoned the sea water so that the next time Scylla bathed in it, she would turn into a revolting sea-creature.

Scylla's fellow monster lurking beneath the opposite cliff was Charybdis, a mythical whirlpool, and daughter of Gaia and Poseidon. She had been thrown by Zeus' thunderbolt into the sea and her voracious appetite required satisfying three times a day, when she would suck in enormous quantities of water and spew it out again.

DOUBLE PERIL

Together, Scylla and Charybdis formed a perilous duo for unwary seamen: if they sailed too close, they were sure to perish. Strangely, Scylla had a disarming puppy-like yelp that belied her true nature. Many unsuspecting victims had strayed too near and been snatched from their boat, and were then crushed by her three sets of gnashing teeth.

Nevertheless, Odysseus felt his chance of survival was better if he favored Scylla, since she could only pluck individual sailors, whereas the whirlpool could swallow a whole boat. In his bid to steer clear of Charybdis, Odysseus went too close to Scylla and the monster

SCYLLA AND GLAUCUS
Scylla rejected the advances of Glaucus, and was turned from a beautiful nymph into a monster.

stretched over the bow and snatched six of his best crew from the deck, one in each mouth, and carried them off to her lair for devouring. Odysseus and the rest of the crew sailed on unscathed.

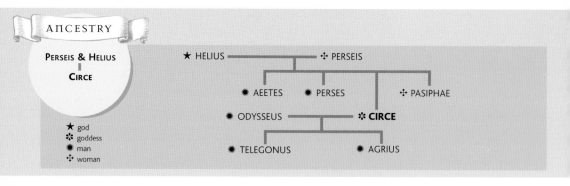

★ HELIUS ——————— ✣ PERSEIS

✳ AEETES   ✳ PERSES   ✣ PASIPHAE

✳ ODYSSEUS ——————— ❊ CIRCE

✳ TELEGONUS   ✳ AGRIUS

CIRCE

Divine enchantress of Odysseus on his voyage home to Ithaca.

As daughter of the Greek sun god Helius, Circe was endowed with great magical powers which she used to transform her enemies, or even those who had just offended her, into animals. When Odysseus' men arrived at her house on the island of Aeaea, they found wolves and lions wandering around. What the Greek voyagers did not realize at first was that these creatures were the victims of Circe's magic.

As soon as the new arrivals were feasted by Circe, who had introduced a powerful drug into the wine, they lost all memory of their native land and turned into swine. Fortunately, one man from the scouting party saw these events from a distance and reported them to Odysseus, who had remained on his ship anchored on the shore.

Undismayed, Odysseus set off to rescue his men, but on the way was lucky enough to meet Hermes, divine protector of travelers. In order to strengthen Odysseus against the magic of Circe, the god gave him a herb that had a black root and a white flower. Hermes also warned him to make Circe promise to behave properly toward her guests.

When Circe discovered that Odysseus was immune to the workings of her drug, she was amazed. Under threat, the enchantress agreed not to harm him and to return his men to human shape. They remained with Circe for a year before she set them a fair wind to set sail from her island.

In Homer's *Odyssey*, Odysseus reflects on the enchantress: "Circe of the lovely tresses, human though she seemed, proved her powers as a goddess by furnishing us with a helpful breeze, which arose astern and filled the sail of our blue-prowed ship." Circe also helped Odysseus by giving him instructions for reaching the Underworld, realm of Hades, where she instructed Odysseus to consult the spirit of the dead seer Tiresias. The Romans identified Circe's island with the promontory Monte Circeo in Italy, and believed that Odysseus stayed there a number of years, fathering three sons by Circe.

CIRCE THE SORCERESS
This ancient relief shows Circe with men whom she had turned into animals.

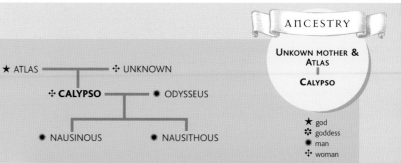
ANCESTRY

UNKOWN MOTHER & ATLAS

CALYPSO

★ god
❖ goddess
✳ man
✛ woman

★ ATLAS ━━━ ✛ UNKNOWN

✛ **CALYPSO** ━━━ ✳ ODYSSEUS

✳ NAUSINOUS ✳ NAUSITHOUS

CALYPSO

Nymph and daughter of Atlas who lived on the island of Ogygie.

Shipwrecked during his epic voyage home from the Trojan War, Odysseus spent seven years on Calypso's island, generally thought to be Gozo, near Malta. Calypso, in Greek meaning "she who conceals," could not believe her luck when this handsome warrior was washed ashore, and she promised him eternal youth if he would stay with her forever. In the first flush of romance, Odysseus was enchanted by her charms, and she bore him two sons, twins by the names of Nausinous and Nausithous. Her home was a huge cavern where she burned roaring fires that scented the air with cedar smoke and thyme. The island was like a paradise, blessed with birdsong, bubbling brooks, and beds of violets and parsley.

In spite of the island's natural beauty, Odysseus became restless and, in time, was desperately unhappy. It is uncertain to what extent he was Calypso's guest or was held as her prisoner. Their love life ceased after a time, and the voyager became homesick. By night he was no longer aroused by Calypso's ardor, while by day he spent his time around the rocks and sandy coves, staring out to sea.

When Zeus sent Hermes with a command for her to send Odysseus away, Calypso protested. But when Hermes reminded her that Zeus had power to compel her compliance, she cooperated by providing Odysseus with materials to build a raft and victuals for the journey ahead: a sack of corn, dried meat,

ODYSSEUS AND CALYPSO
Calypso lived on a wondrous island, and made her home in an enormous cave filled with natural riches. Odysseus and Calypso lived happily on her island for years before he became homesick and restless. Calypso eventually helped the traveler to go home.

wine, and water. She also gave him an axe and various other tools—so much help, in fact, that he suspected her of trickery. But when the day came to depart, he bid her farewell and set sail on a favorable wind.

INDEX

Note: Rom. indicates the Roman equivalent.

CREDITS

Key: l, left r, right

1, 46l, 73 *Psyche brought to life by Eros' kiss* (1793) Antonio Canova © The Art Archive/Musée du Louvre Paris/Dagli Orti; **2, 25, 127** *Leda and the swan* (c.1515) Leonardo da Vinci © The Art Archive/Galleria Borghese Rome/Dagli Orti(A); **3, 128** *Helen and Menelaus* (c.520 bc) Pamphaios © The Art Archive/Musée du Louvre Paris/Dagli Orti; **4, 66** *Apollo, Minerva and the 9 Muses* © The Art Archive/Antiquarium Castellamare di Stabia Italy/Dagli Orti; **5, 132** *Achilles and Ajax, Athena behind* (c.515 bc) © The Art Archive/Musée du Louvre Paris/Dagli Orti; **6** *View of Olympus* (1530) Giulio Romano © The Art Archive/Palazzo del Te Mantua/Dagli Orti(A); **8, 22** *Saturn devouring child* (1636–40) Peter Paul Rubens © The Art Archive/Museo del Prado Madrid/Dagli Orti(A); **10** *Chaos* (1655) © Bettmann/Corbis; **11** *Thalassa and Gaia suckling children*, (12th cent.) © The Art Archive/San Zeno Maggiore Verona Italy/Dagli Orti(A); **12** *Uranus* (1828) Karl F. Schinkel © Bettmann/Corbis; **13** *Bearded cyclops* © The Art Archive/Musée de la Civilisation Gallo-Romaine Lyons/Dagli Orti; **14** *Furies Before Gates of Dis* (1861) Dore © Chris Hellier/Corbis; **15** *Destiny or the Fates* (c.1820) Francisco de Luciente Goya © The Art Archive/Museo del Prado Madrid/Dagli Orti(A); **16** *Night* (c.1560–65) Johan Gregor Van der Schardt © V&A Images/Victoria and Albert Museum; **17** *The Judgement of Paris* (1548) Frans Floris © Museumslandschaft Hessen Kassel/The Bridgeman Art Library; **18** *Nemesis* (2nd–3rd cent. AD) © The Art Archive/National Museum Damascus, Syria/Dagli Orti; **19** *Stele dedicated to Saturn*, from El-Ayaida, 323 AD, Roman © Musee National du Bardo, Le Bardo, Tunisia, Giraudon/The Bridgeman Art Library; **22, 106, 112** *The Apotheosis of Hercules* (1733–36) Francois Lemoyne © The Art Archive/Dagli Orti; **24** *Zeus and Semele* (c.1740) Luca Ferrari © The Art Archive/Museo di Castelvecchio Verona/Dagli Orti(A); **26** *The Birth of the Milky Way* (1637) Peter Paul Rubens © The Art Archive/Museo del Prado Madrid; **28** *Neptune on a Horse* (c.1610) Werner Jacobsz van den Valckert © Christie's Images/Corbis; **30** Demeter, marble copy of 4th-cent. original © The Art Archive/Dagli Orti; **31** *Hestia*, (detail) © The Art Archive/Archaeological Museum Tarquinia/Dagli Orti; **32** Mars, from forum of Augustus (2nd cent. AD) © The Art Archive/Musée du Louvre Paris/Dagli Orti; **33** *Vulcan and Venus* (c.1625) Mortlake Tapestry Factory © V&A Images/Victoria and Albert Museum; **34** *Pallas Athena* (1898) Franz von Stuck © Ali Meyer/Corbis; **36** *The Chariot of Apollo* (1787) Bernardino Galliari © The Art Archive/Galleria Sabauda Turin/Dagli

Orti; **38** *Diana's Hunt* (1617) Domenico Zampieri Domenichino © The Art Archive/Galleria Borghese Rome/Dagli Orti(A); **40** *The Birth of Venus* (c.1485) Sandro Botticelli © The Art Archive/Galleria degli Uffizi Florence/Dagli Orti(A); **44l, 54** *Head of Medusa* (16th cent.) Flemish School © The Art Archive/Galleria degli Uffizi Florence/Dagli Orti; **44** *Mercury and Argus* (1659) Diego Velazquez © The Art Archive/Museo del Prado Madrid; **44r, 67** *The Rape of Persephone* (1622) Gian Lorenzo Bernini © Massimo Listri/Corbis; **45** *Venus and Vulcan*, Giulio Romano (d.1546) © The Art Archive/Musée du Louvre Paris/Dagli Orti; **46r, 63** *Asclepius* © Mimmo Jodice/Corbis; **47, 72** *Greek silver decadrachma coin* (c.460 bc) © The Art Archive; **48** From *Voyage of Saint Louis into Purgatory*, from San Patrizio (c.14th cent. AD) © The Art Archive/Museo Correr Venice/Dagli Orti; **49** *Perseus and the Graiae* (1877) Sir Edward Burne-Jones © Southampton City Art Gallery, Hampshire, UK/The Bridgeman Art Library; **50** *Harness ornament, silver gilt, Thracian* © The Art Archive/Archaeological Museum Sofia/Dagli Orti; **51** *Thetis immerses son Achilles in River Styx* (18th cent. AD) Antoine Rogat Borel © The Art Archive/Galleria Nazionale Parma/Dagli Orti(A); **52** *Charon crossing the Styx* (c.1524) Joachim Patinir © The Art Archive/Museo del Prado Madrid/Dagli Orti; **53** *Winged Victory of Samothrace* (c.190 bc) © The Art Archive/Musée du Louvre Paris/Dagli Orti(A); **56** *Ulysses and the Sirens* (3rd cent. AD) © The Art Archive/Bardo Museum Tunis/Dagli Orti; **57** *Sea centaurs and nereids* (3rd cent. AD) © The Art Archive/Archaeological Museum Tipasa Algeria/Dagli Orti; **58** *Helios in Chariot* © Araldo de Luca/Corbis; **59** *Aurora* (c.1920 AD) Adolfo de Carolis © The Art Archive/Galleria d'Arte Moderna Piacenza; **60** *Endymion* by Guercino © Arte & Immagini srl/Corbis; **61** *Blind Orion Searching for the Rising Sun* (c.1658) Nicholas Poussin © The Metropolitan Museum of Art; **62** *Zeus, Leto, Apollo and Artemis* (c.400 AD) © The Art Archive/Harper Collins Publishers; **64** *Orpheus and Eurydice* (17th cent.) Peter Paul Rubens © The Art Archive/Museo del Prado Madrid; **68** *The Tortures of Tantalus*, (17th cent. AD) Flemish School © The Art Archive/Bibliothèque des Arts Décoratifs Paris; **69** *Hercules or Sisyphus* (4th cent. BC) The Art Archive/Archaeological Museum Naples/Dagli Orti; **70** *Bacchus and Ariadne* (1523) Titian (Tiziano Vecellio) © The Art Archive/National Gallery London/Eileen Tweedy; **74** *Pandora Opening the Box* (c.1800) Walter Crane © Bettmann/Corbis; **75** *Pandora* (19th cent. AD) Masquelier © The Art Archive/Culver Pictures; **76** *Prometheus* (1549) Titian (Tiziano Vecellio) © The Art Archive/Museo del Prado Madrid/Dagli Orti; **78** *Triumph of Galatea* Francesco Podesti (1800–95) © Art Archive/Galleria d'Arte

Moderna Rome/Dagli Orti; **79** *Atlas*, Jacopo Zucchi © Massimo Listri/Corbis; **80** *Aphrodite of the Sandal* (c.100 bc) © The Art Archive/National Archaeological Museum Athens/Dagli Orti; **81** *Chiron and Achilles* © The Art Archive/Archaeological Museum Naples/Dagli Orti; **82, 138** *Aeneas fleeing Troy* (1753) Pompeo Batoni © The Art Archive/Galleria Sabauda Turin/Dagli Orti; **84, 89** *The Dioscuri* (detail) (c. 6th cent. bc) © The Art Archive/Museo Nazionale Palazzo Altemps Rome/Dagli Orti; **86** *Jason and the Golden Fleece*, Erasmus Qeellinus (1607–78) © The Art Archive/Museo del Prado Madrid/Dagli Orti(A); **88** *Thetis carried off by Peleus* © The Art Archive/Bibliothèque des Arts Décoratifs Paris/Dagli Orti; **90** *Meleager and Atalanta* (1731) Bernard Picart © Historical Picture Archive/Corbis; **91** *Medea and Jason with Their Sons* (1st cent. AD) © Mimmo Jodice/Corbis; **92, 98** Minos, King of Crete (1861) Gustave Dore © Chris Hellier/Corbis; **94** *Cadmus* © Adam Woollfitt/Corbis; **96** *The Rape of Europa* (1747) François Boucher © The Art Archive/Musée du Louvre Paris/Dagli Orti(A); **97** *Wounded Amazon pursued by Greek soldier* (2nd cent. BC) © The Art Archive/Archaeological Museum Piraeus/Dagli Orti; **100** *The Fall of Icarus* (1637) Jacob Peter Gowy © The Art Archive/Musée du Louvre Paris/Dagli Orti; **102** *Theseus and the Minotaur* © Mimmo Jodice/Corbis; **103** *Bacchus and Ariadne* (18th cent. AD) Sebastiano Ricci © National Gallery Collection, by kind permission of the Trustees of the National Gallery, London/Corbis; **104** *Ariadne in Naxos* (c.1510) Master of the Campana Cassoni © Musee du Petit Palais, Avignon, France, Peter Willi/The Bridgeman Art Library; **108** *Perseus holding up head of the Gorgon Medusa* (17th cent. AD) Annibale Carracci © The Art Archive/Dagli Orti; **109** *Perseus and Andromeda* (17th cent. AD) Giuseppe Cesare © Archivo Iconografico, S.A./Corbis; **110** *Danae receiving the shower of gold*, Titian (Tiziano Vecellio) (1487–1576) © The Art Archive/Museo del Prado Madrid/Dagli Orti; **111** *Bellerophon on winged horse Pegasus from the Heraklion of Thasos* (540–500 bc) © The Art Archive/Archaeological Museum Thasos/Dagli Orti(A); **114, 116** *Oedipus (Theban hero) solves riddle of the Sphinx* (1808) Jean Dominique Ingres © The Art Archive/Musée du Louvre Paris/Dagli Orti(A); **118** *Oedipus killing his father Laius, king of Thebes* © The Art Archive/Egyptian Museum Cairo/Dagli Orti; **119** *The case of Jocasta, Queen of Thebes*, folio 12 of 15th cent. manuscript of Boccaccio's *On the Fates of Famous Men* © The Art Archive/Bibliothèque Inguimbertine Carpentras/Dagli Orti; **120** *Ulysses invoking the shade of Tiresias*, Edme Bouchardon (d.1762) © The Art Archive/Musée du Louvre Paris/Dagli Orti; **121** *Sphinx* © Moira Clinch; **124** *Judgement of Paris* (16th cent. AD) Flemish school © The Art Archive/Museo

Civico Udine/Dagli Orti(A); **125** *Head of Paris* (c.1810) Antonio Canova © Araldo de Luca/Corbis; **122, 126** *Head of Helen* (detail) Antonio Canova © Mimmo Jodice/Corbis; **129** *Mask* (16th cent. BC) © The Art Archive/National Archaeological Museum Athens/Dagli Orti; **130** *Triumph of Achilles* (1815) Antonio Calliani © The Art Archive/Royal Palace Caserta Italy/Dagli Orti; **133** *Briseis Brought to Achilles*, Peter Paul Rubens (1577–1640) © Archivo Iconografico, S.A./Corbis; **134** *Chariot Race*, Greek School (5th cent. BC) © Archaeological Museum, Olympia, Archaia, Greece, Alinari/The Bridgeman Art Library; **135** *Diomedes* (1865) Gustave Moreau © The Art Archive/Musée des Beaux Arts Rouen/Dagli Orti; **136** *The Death of Priam* (1785) Regnault, Jean-Baptiste © Musée de Picardie, Amiens, France, Giraudon/The Bridgeman Art Library; **137** *Hector, tied to a chariot*, (2nd cent. AD) © The Art Archive/National Museum Beirut/Dagli Orti; **138** *Sibyl* (1511) Michelangelo Buonarroti © Alinari Archives/Corbis; **140, 143** *Troilus, son of Priam* (c.535 bc) © The Art Archive/National Archaeological Museum Athens/Dagli Orti; **141** *The Sacrifice of Iphigenia* (c.79 AD) © Mimmo Jodice/Corbis; **142** *Cassandra* (17th cent. AD) © Stapleton Collection/Corbis; **144** *Orestes and Pylades in Tauris* © The Art Archive/Dagli Orti; **145** *Sacrifice of Iphigenia* (1757) © The Art Archive/Villa Valmarana Vicenza Italy/ Dagli Orti; **146** *Orestes and Electra* (1st cent. bc) © The Art Archive/Museo Nazionale Palazzo Altemps Rome/Dagli Orti; **147** *Death of Dido*, Antoine Coypel (1661–1722) © The Art Archive/Musée Fabre Montpellier/Dagli Orti; **148, 154** *Ulysses and Polyphemus*, (c.1551) Tibaldi Pellegrino © The Art Archive/Palazzo Poggi Bologna/Dagli Orti; **150** *Athena disguises Greek hero Ulysses as beggar*, Giuseppe Bottani (c.1765) © The Art Archive/Civiche Racc d'Arte Pavia Italy/Dagli Orti(A); **152** *Penelope weaving on her loom* (c.1505) from *La Vie des Femmes Celebres*, by Antoine du Fou © The Art Archive/Musée Thomas Dobrée Nantes/Dagli Orti; **153** *Telemachus*, Alessandro Ciccarelli © The Art Archive/Museo di Capodimonte, Naples/Dagli Orti(A); **155** *Glaucus and Scylla* (1581) Bartholomaeus Spranger © Archivo Iconografico, S.A./Corbis; **156** *Circe and men with animal heads* (3rd cent. AD) © The Art Archive/Museo Civico Orvieto/Dagli Orti; **157** *Cave with Odysseus and Calypso* Brueghel, Jan the Elder (d.1625) © Johnny van Haeften Gallery, London/The Bridgeman Art Library

All other images are the copyright of Quarto Publishing plc. While every effort has been made to credit contributors, Quarto would like to apologize should there have been any omissions or errors— and would be pleased to make the appropriate correction for future editions of the book.